Robin Williams

Biography

The humorous soul of a comedian

Kathryn M Schneider

Legal Notice:

Disclaimer Notice:

Please keep in mind that the information in this document is only for educational and entertainment purposes. Every effort has been made to present accurate, up-to-date, reliable, and comprehensive information. There are no express or implied warranties. Readers understand that the author is not providing legal, financial, medical, or professional advice. This book's content was compiled from a variety of sources. Please seek the advice of a licensed professional before attempting any of the techniques described in this book. By reading this document, the reader agrees that the author is not liable for any direct or indirect losses incurred as a result of using the information contained within this document, including, but not limited to, errors, omissions, or inaccuracies.

CONTENTS

Chapter 1.

A MUCH - LOVED MAN

The globe was in shock on August 11, 2014. Robin Williams, the Oscar-winning actor, comedian, and all-around comic genius, was discovered dead at his home in Tiburon, California, just outside of San Francisco. He was only sixty-three years old. Was it a heart attack or a stroke that had occurred? He hadn't been seen much in public recently, but no one outside his immediate group was aware that something was seriously wrong.

However, it soon became evident how mistaken he was. For this was not a catastrophic medical situation; rather, it appeared that the talented but troubled comedian had committed himself. A statement was issued by the Marin County Sheriff's Office. '[It] assumes the death was caused by asphyxia,' it said. Williams, in other words, had hanged himself. The world was shocked: Robin Williams was not only a well-known actor, but also a beloved one. Generations had grown up watching his films, and he was also known to be compassionate and generous in his personal life. Yes, he'd had well-publicised issues with drugs and alcoholism in the past, but despite a recent stint in recovery, it was widely assumed that he was rid of his afflictions. This appears to be false now.

More information began to emerge. More information was available from the Marin County Sheriff's Office. It had received a 911 call at 11.55 a.m. Pacific time from a guy who was 'unconscious and not breathing inside his apartment,' it said. At 12:02 p.m., Robin Williams was pronounced deceased.

The entire statement was as follows:

On August 11, 2014, at around 11:55 a.m., Marin County Communications received a 9-1-1 call stating that a male adult had been discovered unconscious and not breathing inside his home in unincorporated Tiburon, CA. The Sheriff's Office, as well as the Tiburon Fire Department and the Southern Marin Fire Protection District, were called to the area, and emergency responders arrived at 12:00 p.m. The deceased male individual has been identified as Robin McLaurin Williams, a 63-year-old resident of rural Tiburon, CA.

The Sheriff's Office's Investigations and Coroner Divisions are currently conducting an investigation into the cause, manner, and circumstances of the death. According to preliminary evidence gathered during the inquiry, Mr. Williams was last seen alive at his home, where he lives with his wife, at 10:00 p.m. on August 10, 2014. Mr. Williams was found shortly before the 9-1-1 call was put to Marin County Communications this morning. At this point, the Sheriff's Office Coroner Division believes the death was caused by asphyxia, but a thorough investigation must be performed before a final conclusion can be reached. A forensic examination is now set for August 12, 2014, followed by toxicology testing.

The rest of the world was in shock, but nothing compared to Williams' family and friends. 'I lost my husband and best friend this morning, while the world lost one of its most beloved artists and beautiful human beings,' his wife, Susan Schneider, said. 'I am completely heartbroken. We respectfully request privacy during this difficult time for Robin's family. We hope that as he is remembered, the focus will be on the numerous moments of joy and laughter he brought to millions.'

And it became evident very quickly that Robin was not in excellent health. '[He] has been suffering from acute depression,' according to his spokesperson, Mara Buxbaum. 'This is a devastating and unexpected loss. The family respectfully requests privacy as they mourn during this difficult time.' His stay in recovery seemed to portend more issues than anyone had anticipated at the time.

Zelda, Robin's twenty-five-year-old daughter, paid a heartfelt tribute. 'Dad was, is, and always will be one of the kindest, most generous, gentlest souls I've ever known, and while there are few certainties right now, one of them is that not just my world, but the entire world, will be a little darker, less colourful, and less full of laughter in his absence. 'We'll just have to work twice as hard to fill it again,' she explained.

His two sons followed suit. 'Yesterday, I lost my father and a best friend, and the world grew a little grayer,' said Zack, his eldest son. Every day, I will carry his heart with me. I would want anyone who loved him to remember him by being kind, kind, and generous in the same way he was. Seek to offer joy to the world, just like he did.'

'There are no words powerful enough to explain the love and respect I have for my father,' Cody, 23, wrote. Without him, the world will never be the same. I shall miss him and carry him with me wherever I go for the rest of my life, and I will long for the day when I will be able to see him again.'

David Steinberg, a fellow comic, had been his manager for 35 years. 'No one made the world laugh quite like Robin Williams,' he remarked. 'I will miss you, my brother, my friend, my soulmate.'

And the tributes were pouring in. 'Robin Williams was an airman, a doctor, a genie, a nanny, a president, a professor, a bangarang Peter Pan, and everything in between,' said US President Barack Obama of the late Robin Williams. 'However, he was one of a kind. He came into our lives as an outsider, but he ended up touching every aspect of the human soul. He cracked us up. He made us all cry. He freely and generously contributed his tremendous talent to those in need, from our warriors stationed abroad to the downtrodden on our own streets. The Obamas express their condolences to Robin Williams' family, friends, and everyone who found their voice and their verse because of him.'

US Secretary of State John Kerry praised his 'extraordinary zest'. 'Robin was a compassionate, involved citizen, not just a big creative talent,' he continued. 'I'll be eternally grateful for his personal friendship and his support for the things that we both really cared about.'

'Robin Williams was a comedy giant, and although we only knew him personally for a season, he was friendly, humorous, and a true professional,' stated 20th Century Fox Television, with whom Robin just created a television series, The Crazy Ones. 'His cast and crew adored him and enjoyed working with him, and our hearts go out to his family and friends. He was truly unique.'

'The talent was legendary,' said David E. Kelley, the show's creator. But it was his kindness and humanity that inspired me the most. A lovely soul who affected all of us. Our hearts are torn because he was such a lovely individual.'

His co-star was Sarah Michelle Gellar. 'Because I knew Robin Williams, my life is a better place,' she told People. 'To my children, he was Uncle Robin; to everyone he worked with, he was the best employer anyone had ever known; and to me, he was not only an inspiration, but the father I had always desired. There aren't enough words to explain the light he was to anybody who had the pleasure of meeting him. Every day, I shall mourn him, but I know his memory will live on. And I thank his family for allowing us to get to know him and see the joy they brought him. We insane people adore you.'

'Our world has lost a comedy genius, a great performer, and a lovely man,' said CBS, which aired the series. We will remember Robin Williams as one of his generation's most unique talents, admired by many, but also as a kind, kind spirit who treated his colleagues and coworkers with tremendous compassion and respect. Our sincere condolences go out to his family, loved ones, and friends.'

Night At The Museum: Secret Of The Tomb, the third instalment of the blockbuster trilogy produced by 20th Century Fox and set to premiere in December 2014, was one of Williams' most recent projects. 'There really are no words to describe Robin Williams' death,' the studio said in a statement. 'He was a cherished member of our community and a member of the Fox family. Our thoughts are with his family, friends, and fans. He'll be sorely missed.'

Robin had received various honours, including two SAG Awards (Screen Actors Guild). 'I am profoundly grieved to learn of Robin Williams' death,' said Ken Howard, president of SAG-AFTRA. He was a performer with boundless range, equally effective at planned and improvised comedy and drama. With his inimitable zany style, he could appeal to mature sensibilities in a stand-up comedy set or make youngsters laugh as Genie in Aladdin. He used his significant talents outside of his work to raise funds for charity. He was not just a gifted individual, but also a great humanitarian. It's a terrible tragedy.'

Williams had also appeared in a number of HBO specials, including ones for Comic Relief. 'Robin Williams graced HBO with his rare abilities for so many years,' the network added. 'He never failed to advance his craft, and he did so with a full, generous, and loving heart. Robin was a prince who was always humble and gracious, and he has a special place in all of our hearts.'

A memorial was erected at the Boston Public Garden bench shown in the film Good Will Hunting. Nicholas Rabchenuk, a lifelong admirer, and his girlfriend went: 'We went to the [Boston] Common and I was pretty disappointed there wasn't anything there,' he told the Hollywood Reporter. The pair decided to change that: they went out to get flowers and chalk, and when they returned, there were four fans sitting on the bench, so the foursome decided to write phrases from the film. Among them were 'Sorry fellas, I went to see about a female' and 'Your move, chief'.

That picture elicited yet another tribute and reminiscence, this time from Minnie Driver, who also appeared in Good Will Hunting.

'I'd gone to watch him and Matt [Damon] film their wonderful sequence on the park bench in Good Will Hunting, and when they paused for lunch, we hung around on the grass eating sandwiches,' she explained to the Hollywood Reporter. 'What started as a riff on something or other to make us and the crew laugh quickly expanded to office workers out on their lunch break, enjoying the sunshine, and pretty soon he stood up and his big beautiful voice, full of laughter, reached out to the people who were now hurrying down from the street and across the park to catch his impromptu stand-up. By the end of lunch, there must have been 200 people listening and laughing. I recall him smiling warmly, patting my shoulder, and saying, "There, now that was GOOD." I adored him and will dearly miss him. My heart goes out to his family and friends.'

Similar tributes began to arise in other places. The marquee at the Laugh Factory on Sunset Boulevard in Los Angeles read, 'Robin Williams Rest In Peace Make God Laugh'. Mork & Mindy, the TV show that had made him famous all those years before, was set in Boulder, Colorado, and admirers came to pay their respects. The lights along the Great White Way went dark for a moment as part of a historic ritual in which Broadway honoured one of its own.

Sally Field, who had previously acted with Williams in Mrs. Doubtfire, was another co-star. 'I'm startled and saddened by Robin,' she told Entertainment Tonight. 'I'm sorry for the comedy world. And how heartbreaking for his family. And I feel bad for Robin. He always lit up when he was able to make others laugh, and he did it his entire life... nonstop. He was a one-of-a-kind individual. There will be no more. Please, God, let him rest in peace now.'

He also appeared in The Birdcage alongside Nathan Lane. 'What I will remember about Robin, perhaps more than his comic genius, remarkable talent, and astounding intellect, was his enormous heart - his tremendous kindness, generosity, and compassion as an acting partner, colleague, and fellow traveller in a harsh world,' Lane added.

Alan Alda described himself as a "Niagara of wit." 'I hope it inspires us all to do something,' he wrote on TIME.com. 'While the entire country and much of the globe mourns his death, can we turn the loss of this artist we adored into something that pushes back against the ravages of despair?'

Chevy Chase, a fellow comic and actor, understood what Williams was going through. 'Robin and I were wonderful friends who shared a little-known disease: depression,' he explained. 'I could never have predicted this finale to his life. I can't believe it. I'm overcome with grief.'

Of fact, Ben Stiller was a co-star (Night At The Museum franchise) and knew him well. 'A tweet cannot begin to capture Robin Williams' heart, spirit, and skill,' he added. 'This is heartbreaking. #RobinWilliams. I met him when I was 13 and a tremendous fan, and he was extremely nice to me, and I observed him to be nice to every fan he ever met... And he was so generous and bright with other actors. Even though he was a genius, he made everyone around him feel important and equal... Even if you didn't know him, what he provided everyone was the same energy in his work, so we all felt it... His influence on the world was enormously favourable. He helped so many individuals. He made myself and a lot of other people laugh for a long time. Because they don't twitter, this message represents all of the Stillers (Jerry, Anne, and Amy) to whom Robin was a close friend. Xxxxx'

Mira Sorvino, who co-starred in The Final Cut, was furious. 'I still can't believe we lost Robin Williams,' she said. 'What a dude, what a comedian. I considered him among my pals and have many fond memories of him. Robin Williams was a sweet, compassionate, generous man who could weave anything and everything into his mind-boggling rants. This should not have happened to Robin, who was a wonderful man. Devastated. 'My heartfelt condolences to his family.'

'I've never known a kinder, brighter, more compassionate person than Robin,' says Old Dogs co-star John Travolta. Robin's dedication as an artist to uplifting our spirits and making us joyful is unparalleled. He adored us all, and we reciprocated.'

The family of the late Christopher Reeve paid a heartfelt tribute. After meeting when they were both students at New York's famous Juilliard School, the American actor and Williams became lifelong friends, and became so close that they were sometimes described as brothers; after Reeve was paralyzed in the aftermath of a riding accident, Robin was quick to visit and spent a lot of time with his old friend until his untimely death in 2004 (in fact, it was Chris's death that was thought to have knocked him off the wagon in the early no. 'Robin's visit to our father's hospital room was the first time Dad actually laughed after his injury,' the family claimed in a statement to People. 'Dad went on to say, "My old friend had helped me know that somehow I was going to be okay." '

Because of the worldwide outpouring of grief and media, Lt. Keith Boyd of the Marin County Sheriff's Office convened a press conference to detail the late actor's dying moments. He'd been discovered hanging. It was revealed that his wife Susan had gone to bed at 10.30 p.m. the previous evening; Robin had gone to sleep in a separate room, and when she left the house the next morning, she had assumed he was still asleep. Sandy Kleinman, a neighbour, observed her go out to walk the dog at 10.30 a.m.

Mara Buxbaum, Williams' publicist, was the one who first noticed anything was wrong when he didn't respond to repeated taps on the door at 11.45 a.m. She entered the room and discovered her client.

Of course, it was too late by then. 'The caller [Buxbaum] was distraught and indicated at that time it was an apparent suicide due to a hanging that had taken place and that rigor mortis had set in,' Boyd said. No one would discuss whether or not a suicide note had been left.

As additional information became available, it became evident that something had gone horribly wrong in recent months. Williams had been sleeping up to eighteen hours a day, complaining of exhaustion and loss of appetite, and had become extremely reclusive. 'He had blackout curtains in his bedroom because Robin didn't want light in there,' a source informed RadarOnline.com. Following his death, photos emerged of him visiting an exhibition at the Bay Area Art Gallery. He appeared uncomfortably thin, even haggard, indicating a serious loss of appetite, which is another indicator of sadness. But there was no visible sign that anything was wrong. Mark Jaeger, the artist whose work was on show that night - Robin had previously purchased one of his works - said that he appeared to be in high spirits that night, laughing constantly and not drinking. The two talked about potential future initiatives. But Williams' dreadfully emaciated look suggested that something was seriously wrong.

Jaeger, a ceramics teacher at Marin Catholic High School in Kentfield, was visibly upset in the aftermath. They met through Robin's wife Susan, an exhibition curator at 142 Throckmorton Theatre, and Williams had been immensely supportive of his work, purchasing a massive clay head from his 'Superhero' series, which showed regular people as superheroes. They had a good talk. 'We were actually discussing putting the superhero notion into a movie script,' Jaeger said to the Marin Independent Journal. 'This idea of a homeless superhero who goes out at night and does good actions and takes care of people in need. "Robin, I'm excited," I said. "Oh, you just jotted down some notes on a piece of paper," he continued, "and I love the idea that it could be a movie but I don't know how to do that." "Then what?" I replied. "Don't worry, I'll take care of it," he said. I'll connect you with the correct individuals, and we can go through this process together, and I'll assist you along the way,'" Jaeger stated. 'He was quite generous. He was always humble when I spoke with him. I'm a nobody, and he made me feel like my job matters.'

Others claimed that Williams was not himself. 'The last time I saw Robin was over the weekend, we'd catch up on the street, just casually,' a non-named neighbour told Mail Online. 'He looked very drawn and emaciated; he didn't resemble the Robin who originally arrived in this village many years ago. He was a shell of himself, fatigued and irritable, but he was still the wonderful guy I had always known. He appeared to be thinking about something. He didn't resemble his stage image; it wasn't the Robin I knew. He was more quiet and down-to-earth than he appeared in the movies. He paid close attention. He was frequently silent and private. He seemed to be in a horrible emotional place the last time I saw him.'

Others mentioned how Robin was much quieter off-screen than on, and how he used to like walking his dogs to be alone with his thoughts. An image of a disturbed and complex man was emerging.

So, what might have triggered such a drastic shift? Williams' persistent difficulties with alcohol, drugs, and depression were now widely known, but many were surprised to learn that he may have also been dealing with major financial issues. This was almost unfathomable in some respects - Robin Williams had been a huge Hollywood A-lister for decades, with a fortune once estimated at £75 million, but he had two very expensive divorces and, while his name was as popular as ever, important film parts weren't coming his way as quickly as they used to. His 600-acre Napa Valley ranch has been on the market for two years, with the asking price reduced from £21 million to £17.8 million, despite him telling pals, 'I just can't afford it anymore.'

Indeed, the financial issues appeared to be quite severe. 'All he could talk about was his significant financial problems. 'During the height of his fame, Robin was renowned for being so kind to his friends and family, and would assist anyone out who needed it,' a family friend told Radar Online. 'There was also irritation expressed by Robin about having to do television and film jobs that he didn't want to take but had to for the paycheck.'

According to reports, he was so concerned about money that he decided to sell off his prized fifty-strong bicycle collection.

Looking at the big picture, there were more indications that something was wrong. The divorces were believed to have cost £20 million, and Williams had openly discussed undertaking another comedy tour, returning to television, and even making low-budget films. 'The movies are wonderful, but a lot of the time they don't even get distribution,' he told Parade magazine in 2013. Divorce is costly. I used to joke that they were going to call it "all the money", but they changed it to "alimony". Your heart is being ripped out through your pocketbook.' He was joking, but many truthful statements are spoken in jest.

Williams was not even living on his ranch at the time of his death; instead, he was living in a Tiburon bungalow that he had acquired from his mother Laurie in 2001. He was talking about having to 'downsize' his life; plainly, money was on his mind.

Others, on the other hand, denied that financial concerns were at the forefront. 'Reports indicating Robin had financial troubles are absolutely wrong,' his spokeswoman Mara Buxbaum told NBC News in an email. 'I appreciate people's desire to comprehend this, but we would advise you to focus on helping others and understanding depression.' Others agreed that the actor had plenty of work coming up and that this was not cause for alarm. Forbes estimates that he was still worth around $50 million. Perhaps not as much as before, but this is not a man on his high horse.

But then something else became clear: not only was poor Robin tortured by a lifetime of demons manifesting themselves in drink and drug troubles, as well as likely money worries and career concerns, but he was also in the early stages of a deadly illness. It may have taken years for the condition to present itself, but Williams was just diagnosed with Parkinson's disease. Could this have been the final straw for him?

Opinions were varied, but his widow, Susan Schneider, felt compelled to make a statement about an illness her husband had refused to make public, as well as to demonstrate that he had not succumbed to drink again. It was written as follows:

Robin devoted much of his life to assisting others. Robin wanted us to laugh and feel less fearful, whether he was entertaining millions on stage, cinema, or television, our warriors on the frontlines, or comforting a sick kid. Since his death, all of us who loved Robin have found solace in the outpouring of love and admiration from the millions of people whose lives he touched. Aside from his three children, his greatest legacy is the joy and happiness he brought to others, particularly those facing personal challenges.

Robin's sobriety was intact, and he was courageous while he battled sadness, anxiety, and the early stages of Parkinson's illness, which he was not yet ready to reveal publicly.

In the aftermath of Robin's untimely death, we hope that others may find the courage to seek the care and assistance they require to treat whatever struggles they are fighting in order to feel less fearful.

It was a daring comment to make at a time when Susan was clearly grieving a great loss. However, it had no effect on the speculation. Williams was an avid biker who took up the sport to assist him overcome his different addictions. Tony Tom, a San Francisco bike store owner and Robin's bicycling buddy who also stated that Robin had utilised cycling to stay off drugs, wondered if the A-lister was scared that as his sickness worsened, he would no longer be able to cycle. Meanwhile, actor and producer Michael J. Fox, who was diagnosed with Parkinson's disease when he was very young, wrote that he was stunned to learn that Robin Williams was a fellow sufferer. He was 'quite sure' Williams' support for his Michael J. Fox Foundation predates the moment he discovered he, too, had the disease, adding, 'A good buddy; I wish him peace.'

With the news out, another option arose: were the medications Williams had been using to treat his disease actually to blame for his overdose? Some folks certainly believed so. Robin had been friends with actor Rob Schneider for nearly twenty years when they both appeared on Saturday Night Live. 'Now that we can talk about it, #Robin Williams was on Parkinson's medication,' he tweeted. Suicide is one among the negative consequences.'

Despite claims that they agreed, the family would not be drawn, albeit a source was willing to speak. 'Robin had just left treatment,' he explained to Forbes. 'He was taking medication for anxiety and sadness, as well as treatments to combat the early symptoms of Parkinson's. Suicidal thoughts are listed as a possible side effect in many of these medications. Many of Robin's acquaintances believe that the cocktail of prescription medicines he was taking played a role in his mental condition deteriorating as soon as it did. Robin had always struggled with melancholy and addiction, but his Parkinson's disease diagnosis and treatment were novel, as was the chemical cocktail he was taking.'

Williams had always been depressed, but Parkinson's diagnosis had made things much worse, and it was widely assumed that depression is also an early indication of the condition. Indeed, the news received so much attention that the National Parkinson Foundation in the United States felt obligated to issue a statement: "We have all been devastated by Robin Williams' death." We are even more heartbroken to learn that he was recently diagnosed with Parkinson's disease. While a diagnosis of any serious condition can be stressful, Parkinson's and depression can coexist. According to a recent NPF study, more than half of persons with the disease suffer from clinical depression, which is a natural component of the disease process. Depression has a greater impact on quality of life than the disease's motor deficits. The National Parkinson Foundation advocates for annual depression screening as an important aspect of treating Parkinson's disease. Depression treatment should include both medicine and counselling. The National Parkinson Foundation urges patients with Parkinson's disease and their families to seek neurologist treatment.

The reverberations persisted. Susan, overwhelmed by grief, abandoned the marital house and the neighbourhood where they shared a home. Williams' children continued to be perplexed and upset.

Zelda tweeted a phrase from Antoine De Saint-Exupéry's French classic The Little Prince: "You - you alone will have the stars as no one else has them... I'll be living in one of the stars. I'll be laughing in one of them. When you look at the sky at night, it will appear as if all the stars are laughing, because you - just you - will have stars that can laugh. I adore you. I'm missing you. I'll keep looking for answers. - Z

It was revealed that the funeral was held relatively quickly: an Episcopalian service, Williams' religion, at Monte's Chapel of the Hills, a funeral home in San Anselmo, California. Following the private funeral, Robin's ashes were dispersed in the San Francisco Bay, which was fitting given that he had resided there since his late teens. As those close to him struggled to make sense of what had happened, there was considerable speculation that it had been a spur-of-the-moment choice, with one close acquaintance noting that he had been discussing forthcoming projects just days before. According to the source, he was 'fully engrossed in the talk' and, as such, didn't appear to be contemplating leaving. However, it was likely not commonly recognized that Williams had a horrific upbringing that had left him damaged for the remainder of his life. He'd played many wounded characters so brilliantly because he, too, was one, and perhaps, ultimately, he was no longer able to withstand the hopelessness that had appeared at regular intervals throughout his life.

A true outpouring of grief was forming: Robin Williams may have been imperfect, but he was a wonderful, kind, and compassionate man, and his premature death was impacting not only his followers, but even others who had previously given him little regard. So, just who was Robin Williams? And how did he come to have such a profound influence on so many individuals all across the world?

Chapter 2.

OH, WHAT A LONELY BOY

The city of Chicago, Illinois. It was the height of summer in Chicago, and Laura McLaurin, a former model from Jackson, Mississippi, and her husband, Ford Motor Company executive Robert Fitzgerald Williams, were overjoyed. Robin McLaurin Williams was born on July 21, 1951. He had two elder half-brothers, Robert Todd Williams (who would become a winemaker known as 'Toad') from his father's first marriage and McLaurin Smith-Williams from his mother's first marriage, but, essentially, Robin was an only child; they all were. 'Todd, myself, and Robin all grew up as only children. My mother's parents adopted me when her first marriage ended in divorce. Todd was raised by his mother. We all get along great. Todd isn't related to me by blood, but we're quite close,' McLaurin, a physics instructor, told the Chicago Tribune in 1991.

Williams undoubtedly came from respectable stock for someone who would have such an anarchic personality: his mother's great grandfather was Mississippi senator and governor Anselm J. McLaurin, and his father came from an exceedingly important Evansville, Indiana family. Robert's father, also named Robert and hailing from Kentucky, was the chief clerk and secretary, treasurer, and general manager of the Indiana Tie Company in 1902. 'He has contributed significantly to the enterprise's success, capably overseeing the interests of the company and managing its trade ties in such a manner that effective results are obtained,' according to the History of the City of Evansville and Vanderburgh County, Indiana. Many of Williams' family relatives are buried in the Evansville cemetery, which sparked tremendous excitement among Robin Williams' Evansville supporters.

But that wasn't the end of it. Robin could proudly claim English, Welsh, Irish, Scottish, German, and French ancestors, which may explain why he was so excellent at dialects later in life. Robin grew up in an affluent family, surrounded by privilege and creature comforts, but he had a neglected life in many ways. When Robin was born, his father was forty-six years old. He was severe and had little time for his young son. Robin's mother was an ambitious model with a wide range of charitable interests outside the home. She, too, was largely absent, and wounds that would never heal began to emerge when he was very small. They would evolve into torments over time, causing him great suffering for the remainder of his life.

Robin grew up in Lake Forest, an affluent neighbourhood north of Chicago. He was not the outgoing comic he would become at the time. The family had a large house, but he spent a lot of time alone, playing with his toys: his father was frequently away on business, and his mother was active in philanthropic work. It doesn't take a psychiatric degree to figure out that the young Robin spent a lot of time trying and failing to get his parents' attention - something that would become a lifelong ambition.

Shy, pudgy, melancholy, and quiet, he was also a nervous child, terrified of shadows and, to be honest, somewhat afraid of his father. It may be cliche to say that many individuals become comedians to deal with their own inner sadness, but Williams' childhood was a textbook example of what drives someone to numb their anguish with alcohol, drugs, and a lot of comedy. As a child, laughter was often in limited supply. 'I had thousands of model soldiers,' he said. 'You learn how to make your own games and read a lot. It wasn't exactly enjoyable, but it eventually helped your range as a comedian and gave you an imagination.'

Nonetheless, he had some pals, and one of them recalls his large collection of toys (almost 2,000 in total). 'I had the usual, olive green plastic army guys, but Robin had this complete setup of hand-painted English soldiers made of lead,' said Jeff Hodgen, who met Williams in fifth grade at Lake Forest's Gorton Elementary School. 'When we initially met, he seemed a little standoffish, but that was simply because he was the new guy at school. I recall once flinging snowballs and colliding with a cop car, which put an end to that. For months following that, every time one of our phones rang at home, we were scared it was the police calling to speak with our parents.' Interestingly, Hodgen stated that Williams was not the class clown, but rather a serious and somewhat quiet young man.

However, life in Lake Forest was pleasant. Despite its proximity to Chicago, it felt more like a tiny city in its own right: being part of the north shore expansion, it had Lake Michigan on one side, where residents could swim in the scorching summers and ice skate in the very cold winters. The large houses, many of which stood on their own plots of land, were designed by some of the twentieth century's most famous architects, including David Adler and Frank Lloyd Wright; the large gardens were ideal for playing in, and children could cycle down the city's wide sidewalks, as they were expected to do - no cycling on the quiet roads. Lake Forest had little problems with poverty or ethnic minorities: the city was mostly white.

Robin transferred to DeerPath Junior High School in the sixth grade after leaving Gorton, but the family relocated to Detroit when he was in the seventh grade, around the age of twelve. Hodgen was taken aback, but he accepted it. 'I missed him, but I had just begun football, so I sucked it up,' he explained.

The family relocated to Bloomfield Hills, at the intersection of Woodward and Long Lake, where Robin subsequently described it as "paradise." 'It was a large, lovely old estate, with a gatehouse, an empty garage with enough for 25 cars, barns, and a very charming old English man, Mr. Williams, who looked after the gardens,' he explained to the Detroit Free Press. 'We didn't own it; we simply rented it. We then relocated to Chicago, and when we returned to Detroit a few years later, we simply rented an apartment. And, you know, it was quite different. But the first house was nice and serene.

There was no one in sight for miles. Only this massive golf course with Tads whacking the old ball.'

In reality, Robin was embellishing the story, whether on purpose or not, because the truth is a little less rosy. He had an entire floor to himself in the attic, surrounded by his massive toy collection, but he didn't like it. He was scared of the shadows and dark nooks. It was a lonely life for a young boy, and while he played on his own, he began to conjure up stories and characters. No one knew they had a comedy genius in their midst at the time: all they saw was a tiny child who wanted to be loved, having been uprooted from a prior existence and now starting over from scratch. 'My imagination was my only companion, my only buddy as a child,' he once stated.

Church was an important aspect of his life. Although his mother was a Christian Scientist, Robin was raised as an Episcopalian. Indeed, he was an active member of the religion for a time, and it became the source of some of his comedy as well as the idea for his role in the 2007 film License to Wed. 'Being a choirboy, and I'm not Catholic, I'm just going back to the old days when I was into going to church and remembering, as a Protestant, which is Catholic light once again, the idea of somebody that could really advise and has something [to] offer,' he told Canmag around the time of the film's release. 'It was simply remembering the folks I grew up with in the Episcopal Church, who taught me that there is no purgatory, only spiritual escrow. That was [the] start of it. Then there's the fact that he's as hands-on as you can be without becoming a priest.'

Robin enrolled at Detroit Country Day School, a private school where he did well in some areas but struggled in others. He became class president, played soccer, and joined the wrestling team, and one of his teachers is claimed to be the inspiration for his character as John Keating in Dead Poets Society. 'I enjoyed school, maybe a little too much,' he told the Washington Post in an interview that corresponded with the premiere of Jack (1996), a film about a youngster who ages four times faster than everyone else that offered a far brighter picture of his early days than reality.

'In high school, I was summa cum laude. That was my motivation. It wasn't simple for me to blend in. I simply went out of my way to blend in. Detroit Country Day was a private boys' school where I played soccer. I was a member of the wrestling team. You know, Mr. All-Around? But I believe what inspired me to play Jack was that innocent time before all of that, riding bikes, making pals in treehouses, and all the other things that blur the line between child and lad. When you're 10, you're still a boy, and that moment right before puberty, which comes around at twelve - or eleven if you live somewhere where the milk is different - is fantastic. A boy is still vulnerable at that age. Boys that age don't have a lot of skill when it comes to masking their emotions. What they are feeling is seen on their faces.'

In reality, some of those boys perceived malevolence. Robin might have liked school, or so he thought, but he had a lot of problems to deal with when he was there, and it was this, combined with his mother's attention and his relative isolation in the family home, that really laid the groundwork for the comedian he would one day become. In another interview, this time with the Oklahoman in 1991, he described life at the time as much more muted. 'I wasn't as animated,' he admitted. 'I went to an all-boys school for around three years. It was similar to the one in Dead Poets Society. Blazer. Motto in Latin. I was constantly pushed about. Not only was there physical bullying, but there was also intellectual bullying. It made me tougher, but it also made me back off a lot. I was wary of interacting with other people. I found a way to bridge the divide through comedy...'

To put it another way, he was being bullied. To begin, he attempted to locate alternate routes home, but this failed. Boys mocked him because he was, in their opinion, tiny, chubby, and well-spoken. He was also dyslexic, which meant he struggled in school and almost certainly had Attention Deficit Disorder (ADHD), neither of which disorders were recognized at the time. Robin couldn't fight back physically, and he couldn't get away from his classmates, so he tried a distraction technique: he started trying to make them laugh. 'I started delivering jokes to keep the shit out of me,' he once admitted, a typical example of the melancholia that lurks beneath so many comedians' grins. Using laughing to defuse conflict? Williams must have understood his abilities would be a double-edged sword from the start.

Robin was not only attempting to impress bullies. He longed to fit in at school, but at home he craved the attention of his parents, especially his mother. As a result, he used the same tactic he used at school: he told jokes.

In an interview with Esquire Magazine, Williams stated, "I'm just beginning to realise that it wasn't always that happy." 'My childhood was somewhat lonely. Quiet. My father was away, and my mother was working and collecting benefits. This woman really raised me, and my mother would come in later, you know, and I knew her, and she was wonderful, charming, and hilarious. But I think comedy began as a way for me to connect with my mother - "I'll make Mommy laugh and that will be okay" - and that's where it began.' In reality, his first impression was of his grandma, marking the beginning of a gift that would distinguish him.

And so it went, the small child desperate to avoid getting pummelling at school and desirous of parental attention at home. And as he proceeded to build coping skills, he began to realise that he truly did have an incredible capacity to make people laugh. But it never quite worked: the family hired maids who looked after Robin, but as much as he adored them, they were no substitute for his mother. As an adult, he admitted to having a severe form of 'Love Me Syndrome' and an extreme fear of abandonment. It wasn't difficult to figure out why. Despite having several pals, he spent his youth alone and isolated. The man who would one day have the entire world eating out of his hand was a bashful, lonely, and terrified little child, and that is what Robin Williams always remained at his core. As someone once said, no amount of money or success can compensate for a bad childhood.

His mother's religiosity didn't help either, albeit he turned it into a source of amusement. 'My mother was a Christian Dior Scientist,' he was insulted. I was bullied not just physically, but also intellectually; people used to kick copies of George Sand in my face.' It was a courageous attempt to conceal past suffering, yet the sadness was clearly there.

There was more turmoil when Robin was approximately sixteen, but this was to be his undoing. As his father Robert became increasingly disillusioned with the automobile industry, the family relocated once more, this time to Woodacre, California, part of Marin County, where Robin would spend the most of his life. He enrolled in Larkspur's Redwood High School. This was not a private school, unlike the last one, and it exposed him to a whole new world. Hawaiian shirts became (and stayed) a part of his wardrobe; he began driving a Land Rover... Life began to open up.

'I came out to California for high school in 1969,' he told the Oklahoman. 'I went to this gestalt high school where one of the instructors once tried LSD. So you walk in and [whispers] "I'm Lincoln." From the formalities of the Midwest to California shortly after the Summer of Love was quite an eye-opener for his anarchist personality. And by this point, his joke-telling had progressed to the point where he was really considering a future in the performing arts.

Indeed, the transfer from the Midwest was most likely instrumental in his development. The Midwest appears to be dominated by pioneer thought despite the fact that it has only been a little more than a century since men risked their lives to bring the land under control. But laid-back California and San Francisco were much different. Williams later stated that he preferred living there because no one appeared to notice him. Of course, this was partly because he had been a long-term local resident and they were used to him, but it also implied that there were already so many quirky residents in that region that he fit right in.

And the same was true at his much more relaxed school, where he was finally free of his tormentors and able to enjoy himself. And, while it was not a private institution, it was nevertheless a good place to study, with many other alumni going on to make their names. One such student was comedian and novelist Greg Behrendt, as was actor David Dukes. Pulitzer Prize-winning New York Times journalist Eric Schmitt, who went on to produce the television version of Teenage Mutant Ninja Turtles. There were also some notable academics, such as Gunnar Carlsson, a mathematics professor at Stanford University, and Don Francis, a well-known US epidemiologist who became a household name in HIV and AIDS research.

Williams' new city had an impression on him from the minute he first saw it. In 2007, he told American Way magazine, "I was sixteen years old." 'My father and mother [as well as myself] had driven across the nation. There was fog pouring in as we drove across the Golden Gate Bridge. I'd never seen fog before. Is that a poisonous gas? No. It's extremely remarkable how it pours over the hills of Marin County and over the Gate. That was my first thought: what is this odd smoke? However, viewing the bridge was extremely lovely. There aren't many things that huge in Detroit. I was particularly impressed by how close to the city there is so much environment. Mount Tamalpais State Park is located in Marin County, California. We have the entire coastline, which is breathtakingly magnificent.'

Overall, it was a new setting that was a pleasant change and provided him with the opportunity to evolve into the man he desired; to explore sport and drama while also relaxing. His father, whom he had always feared, may have become more calm as well. After all, he was retired now, out of the business world and able to relax in a way he had never really done before. (That said, Williams never really spoke a great deal about his father, other than to recollect the moment when he launched into him for buying a Japanese car rather than an American one. So maybe relaxation never came.)

Laurie, his mother, surely observed the difference in her son. 'As a child, Robin was really bashful,' she told the Chicago Tribune. 'His father was stern, and I believe Robin's turning moment came when he left Detroit Country Day School, which was a lot of boys wearing extremely proper white shirts, and we moved to Marin. He enrolled at Redwood High School and began bringing home some fairly wild and woolly pals. They wouldn't have been drawn to him if he hadn't been a little wild himself. Later, his involvement with the Committee [an improv comedy troupe] was quite thrilling for him. People would shout out a single line, and he was great at improvising from that.'

She was well aware of her son's brilliance, even if she never fully realised that much of it was done to impress her. Eventually, the lonely youngster who impersonated his grandma to make his mother laugh grew into an international star, and she was quite proud of it. 'I believe Robin was sent here to make us laugh,' she concluded. 'You know, I'm told that at Yale Drama School, Robin and Steve Martin are great instances of the fool in a king's court. The fool must be bright, well-informed, and capable of making the monarch laugh without having his head severed. That would be Robin.'

And it was, since he was to become the Court Jester, piercing the pomposity of the great and good while always getting away with it. It should not be forgotten that Williams possessed not only amazing brilliance but also remarkable charm. Even when he was at his craziest, there was never a sense that he was meant to hurt anyone

27

with his comedy: if anything, the only person he looked to be wanting to hurt was himself. And it all originated from his early years of loneliness - he had been brutally damaged himself, and the pain had never left him.

But he was considerably happy now than he had been earlier, rattling around a large mansion on his lonesome. He told American Way magazine, "We lived in Tiburon, in this little house." 'In Tiburon, there's a terrific restaurant called Sam's Anchor Cafe, which is still open. My father liked this seafood restaurant because you could dine outside on warm days or inside. It's just an old-fashioned seafood and hamburger joint, and my father adored the hamburgers.'

However, in Robin's relationship with his mother, the humour remained, on some level, associated with childhood. Although the rest of the world perceived him as an adult, the relationship between mother and child never really grew beyond that, and despite his age, Williams still operated on some fundamental level with his mother as if he were still a child.

'He's really excellent at voices, you know,' she added. 'He can play a small child quite effectively. I'll be hurrying out the door one day when I get this call [small girl's voice]: "Hello, this is Candy. My mother is not at home. "May I join you in your game?" And I feel impatient; he can still trick me. He also has a key to my house, and when I call, he answers the phone and pretends to be the housekeeper, telling me that Mrs. Williams has gone away.'

This does not appear to be fully healthy. Indeed, even having his mother's attention in later years, Robin would never be able to escape the hardships of early life and the urge to make his mother laugh. But now that he was in high school and no longer being bullied, he was starting to grow. He kept up with athletics - he even considered going pro for a short period and excelled as a runner, another pastime that wound up in his stand-up act when he equated the famous 'runners' high' to being high on drugs - joined the drama club, and began to find his feet. Sharp-witted as ever, there was no need to try to outwit the bullies by now, but he couldn't stop himself from amusing his classmates nevertheless. In later life, he stated that he had only taken up acting to get laid.

Williams, on the other hand, was not your average jock. Following his death, a fellow student was asked if it was true that he used to start every day with the cry, 'Good morning, Redwood High!' (an improbable situation, to say the least). His classmate's response was unequivocal: 'No way. C'mon. Nobody does things like that. That man was a total nerd. He wore bow ties and was extremely quiet. He was never one of my favourites.'

However, others did. He had friends now, people he could hang out with, and he was going to meet others with whom he would be friends for the rest of his life. In 1967, William Drew met Williams at Redwood High School. In the aftermath of his death, he told the BBC, 'I remember Rob and I taking a cool-down lap after track practice.'As we passed the shot putters, Rob abruptly came to a halt, stepped over to the pit, looked over the three enormous guys chucking the shot, picked up one of the heavy steel balls, and, well, use your imagination on Robin Williams' comment. In Drama Club, no screenplay was safe, and no line was holy. Robin may be summed up in two words: passion and compassion. He was devoted and passionate about all he did, and he was compassionate about others, as he exhibited in his senior years.'

However, it was time to move on, to begin planning for the future and deciding what to do next. Despite a reportedly difficult childhood, Williams was coming into his own in his late teens, already highly clever and good at making people laugh. But it wasn't evident that this would be the turning point in his life, not just as an individual, but also as a performer. His peers had no idea what to make of it all. Will he make it in the great, wide world in whatever role he chooses? His classmates picked him 'funniest' and 'least likely to succeed' at graduation - they were clearly incorrect on both counts.

Chapter 3.

ROBIN AND THE JUILLIARD

Robin Williams was, if not a natural showman, then one who had been shaped by the ups and downs of his youth. But the penny had not yet dropped. So he enrolled in 1969 at Claremont Men's College in Claremont, California, to study political science. But it wasn't what he was supposed to do, and it didn't last. He was only there for one semester, and depending on who you believe, he either dropped out because he realised he'd made a mistake or was expelled for smashing a golf cart into the dining hall. He had done some acting during his time there and was increasingly being asked to follow that particular star. He didn't last, whatever the reality was.

His father wasn't delighted, but he handled it well enough. He did, however, advise his kid to learn a real job, such as welding, just to be safe. Robin did attend a class, but his instructor was not encouraging: 'You can become blind from this,' he said. It was not the happiest of times.

To anyone with half a brain, it was becoming increasingly clear that Robin wasn't just talented; he was amazing; he completely stood out. Even at this early juncture in his career, he was demonstrating a wit, an ability to improvise, and a comedic gift that was unusual for someone so young. All of those early aspects were present, of course - the fight against bullying, the need to capture his mother's attention, the loneliness that drove him to rely on his imagination - but there was something more. Williams has unique skills, which are now beginning to emerge.

Claremont Men's College and a career in politics were out of the question. A quick rethink was required. So he ended up at the

College of Marin in Kentfield, California, to study drama for the next three years. It was a community college, where students did not get degrees but instead pursued disciplines that fell halfway between high school and university. His anarchist side had been fully unleashed. Fellow students recall him performing ridiculous walks around campus in green shorts and a swimming cap. (This was around the time Monty Python would have been on British television, and many budding comedians were doing their own ridiculous walks.)

According to his theatrical professor, James Dunn, he stood out from the start. It was a character in a Dickens adaptation that rapidly distinguished him. And, as time passed, it was his ability to improvise that truly distinguished him. 'When he played Fagin in Oliver!I realised he was more gifted than the other youngsters!' Dunn told the Marin Independent Journal immediately after Williams died. 'We were having light board problems and had barely made it halfway through the musical by midnight. At one point, he began talking to a baton he was carrying, and the baton responded. It relieved the tension, and he had everyone in stitches. At 2 a.m., I called my wife and told her that this young man was going to be something extraordinary.'

Friends recall him as Malvolio in Shakespeare's Twelfth Night, in addition to his role as Fagin. Critics who believe he should have stayed in stand-up comedy and avoided serious acting may be astonished to hear that his acting passion was present from the beginning. Williams, on the other hand, would utilise the legendary soliloquies as inspiration for some extended improvisation of his own. Although, notwithstanding his subsequent comments regarding his former student, many pupils thought that Dunn's patience was stretched at times. He did, however, enjoy his student's extraordinary vitality, especially when it expressed itself in the early hours. Dunn held a 24-hour fundraiser every year, with his pupils participating in various capacities. Robin would show up at 2 or 3 a.m., no matter how late it was, and begin his performance.

Indeed, he did not stop anytime he was on exhibit in public. He drove a tiny Volkswagen Beetle to the Trident restaurant on Sausalito's waterfront. He worked there as a server to fund his education, and even there he would put on a sideshow, juggling plates and glasses and whatever else came to hand while entertaining the guests with an impromptu comedic routine. Marin has never seen anything like it! Off duty, he was nothing like that because he was shy. Many people said after his death that when he was not on stage, he was totally different: not a joker and, in many ways, extremely introverted. Robin lived 'in a dark place,' according to a friend, and this was also accurate at the time.

But that didn't stop him from practising his routine. When he wasn't in college or working as a waiter, Williams was making his way around the local comedy clubs, starting with Holy City Zoo, where he worked his way up from bartender to performing on stage. The name Holy City Zoo comes from its first owner, Robert Steger, who obtained a sign for free at a closing-down sale at a zoo in Holy City, California. (Williams was once claimed to 'use the club as his neighbourhood rehearsal place.') It was a tiny facility in San Francisco's Richmond neighbourhood, seating only 78 people and selling beer, wine, and soft drinks. It was formerly a folk music club. However, the management started hosting open-mic evenings for comedians on Sundays, which proved so popular that they were expanded to the rest of the week.

This was where Robin could start developing his craft in a safe, small setting with individuals he knew. He had a far longer history of formal training than most people realised, but this and other San Francisco comedy clubs were where he developed his profession. (In fact, after he got renowned, he returned to Holy City Zoo, albeit he was always careful to let the other acts go on before him. It's just as well... He would have been a difficult act to follow.)

Holy City Zoo closed its doors for the first time in 1984, however it would reopen later that year. 'I'm sad,' Robin admitted. 'We had fantastic moments here, bizarre times here; this wasn't a haven, it was a game preserve,' she says. I recall a large black guy coming in with a baseball bat and saying, "I'd like to audition."" However, much of that is in the past. There have been so many changes.'

When the club finally closed for good in 1993, he was as depressed as many of its former members: it was "like someone turning off your aunt's life support." It's really depressing. The Zoo served as the womb.'

Steve Pearl, a comedian, witnessed Williams perform there. He was a 'tornado, frantic, and tearing all over the stage,' Pearl said in a tribute to Williams in The New Yorker. 'It both inspired and frightened me.' He was also starting to make his own money by this point. He was known for his great generosity throughout his life, and it was immediately at the start, when he was earning almost nothing while working at Holy City Zoo, that he became aware of a friend's gambling debt. He paid it back.

He also appeared at The Boarding House and the Old Spaghetti Factory. The Boarding House was another comedy hotspot: it was where Steve Martin recorded his first three albums and where Dolly Parton and Talking Heads performed. The Old Spaghetti manufacturer began as a pasta manufacturer before being converted into a restaurant with cabaret performances. It, too, hosted several incredibly famous names, including Beat Generation pioneers Jack Kerouac and Allen Ginsberg, as well as Ken Kesey (author of One Flew Over the Cuckoo's Nest). The entire environment was quite dynamic, and Williams was a big part of it. He was beginning to gain a following by this point, with fans seeking out his performances. Almost definitely, he didn't need what came next because he was doing so well and was well on his path to success, but the young Robin was full of ambition and anxious to join one of the greatest performing-arts schools in the country.

He was already on his way up, but now he's officially in the big leagues. In 1973, he received a full scholarship to The Juilliard School in New York after three years at Marin. He was one of just twenty students to be accepted into the Advanced Programme that year, and one of only two to be accepted by John Houseman, who was the first to recognize his true potential. The other student was Christopher Reeve, better known as Superman, who would go on to become a longtime friend. William Hurt, an American theatrical and film actor, was another classmate. 'He wore tie-dyed shirts with tracksuit bottoms and talked a mile a minute,' Reeve said of his pal later. 'I'd never seen that much energy in one individual before. He was like an untethered balloon that had been inflated and then let go. I stood there in astonishment as he caromed off the walls of the classrooms and halls. To say he was "on" would be an understatement.

This was a dramatic improvement in Williams' fortunes. The Juilliard School of Music is one of the world's most prestigious performing-arts institutions. It is exceedingly difficult to get into and boasts a considerable proportion of the crème de la crème of the American performing industry as graduates. It is based at the Lincoln Center for Performing Arts in New York. Dance, drama, and music were all taught there, and getting a spot was as sure as anyone could be in the volatile showbiz business that you were cut out to succeed.

Despite being a school for actors rather than comedians, Robin's future comedy was greatly influenced by his time at Juilliard. He came from an educated, wealthy, and intellectual family, but The Juilliard provided him with an additional layer of education, reference, and information. Because Williams could be so frenetic on stage, as well as because he became embroiled in the 1970s drugs scene and was so much a part of our mainstream culture, it's easy to ignore how well educated and thoroughly read he was. He already knew Shakespeare, but The Juilliard School taught him so much more: he was a man who could recite a Shakespeare soliloquy for hours before straying off on a tangent and talking about drugs. Some people were snobbish about Williams' mainstream acting career; he was a classically trained, highly educated actor who also seemed to have a manic side.

He caught the eye of John Houseman, the Romanian-born British-American actor who had previously worked extensively with Orson Welles and was well regarded for his role as Professor Charles Kingsfield in the 1973 film The Paper Chase. He was a titan of the performing arts world, both in film and theatre, and the founding director of The Juilliard Drama Division. His other protégés included actor and comedian Kevin Kline, actress and singer Patti LuPone, and actor, tenor, voice artist, and comedienne Mandy Patinkin. Williams' experiences at Juilliard were varied, as discussed further below, although he clearly profited from his collaboration with Houseman.

He and Christopher Reeve shared a room at The Juilliard, and it was here that they formed a relationship that lasted until Christopher's tragic and early death from cardiac arrest in 2004. 'He is SO excellent, and such a method actor, that Oliver Sacks wanted to connect him up to an EEG to check if he genuinely mimicked the brainwaves of the actual patients,' Robin said of his friend. 'No joke,' he remarked in a Reddit interview published in 2013. "He was such a fantastic buddy to me at Juilliard, physically feeding me because I didn't think I had money for food or my student loan hadn't come in yet, and he would share his food with me," she says. The two young men agreed that whichever of them grew more successful would assist the other. In the end, both became prosperous around the same time, but their friendship remained strong, with Williams continuing to play a significant role in Reeve's life following his catastrophic riding accident. It was rumoured that he financially supported the family, possibly as a modest reward for all that shared food.

Kelsey Grammer (of Cheers and Frasier fame) and Diane Venora, who received a Golden Globe nod and a New York Film Critics Award for her portrayal in Clint Eastwood's Bird, a portrait of jazz great Charlie Parker, were among her students. Diane told the Los Angeles Times, "We were in the same class for four years." 'He was bright and multifaceted, extremely sensitive, with a sensitivity and humility that gave his art enormous power. I was madly in love with him.'

Christopher Reeve also praised his friend's rising skill. 'Robin and I were third year students,' he told New York Magazine in 1993. We were assigned to special advanced sections, and we were frequently the only pupils in a class. Robin threw the teachers off because John Houseman had a vision of what a Juilliard actor should be - beautifully spoken but a little homogenised. He performed a Beyond the Fringe monologue that had us laugh so hard we were in physical pain; they stated it was "a comedy bit, not acting."

But Robin was fantastic at the 'comic bit,' and he simply got better and better. A peer was Robert M. Beseda, who became assistant dean of drama at North Carolina School of the Arts. He told Time Warner Cable News, "We were classmates." 'He was a year my junior. I didn't know him well; he was too cool for someone like me, but he was hilarious. He presided over the proceedings and had us all in stitches. I remember him from a Midsummer Night's Dream workshop. He was Thisbe, and he had two grapefruits under his dress as breasts when the Mechanicals performed their play in Act V. They suddenly appeared at one point, and he began to juggle them. It was one of the funniest sight gags in comic history. It's something I'll never forget. He is a profound loss to a world that desperately needs what he so generously provided us!'

Meanwhile, New York stood in stark contrast to San Francisco. The laid-back Pacific city was nothing like the teeming metropolis where Williams now lived, home to Broadway, where he would later perform, and one of the world's most vibrant and exciting places. It was his first time living on his own as an adult (albeit with Reeve), and it was the first time he was free of his parents and able to live on his own terms, but the old demons remained.

People were captivated by his comedy, particularly the manic element, but none of them truly understood what lay behind it: a bullied boy reaching out to an absentee mother. He was learning to build a shell and channel his pain elsewhere, but even the excitement of The Juilliard and New York City couldn't completely erase the pain. It wouldn't be long before he sought other methods of erasing it, but for the time being, he was learning quickly. To make some money, he and a friend performed a white-faced mime sequence in front of the Metropolitan Museum of Art, earning themselves $75 one day - a decent sum back then.

Edith Skinner, a leading voice and speech coach, was one of Robin's (and Christopher's) teachers, and she taught them how to speak in different dialects. She soon discovered that Robin could do it without any outside assistance. Michael Kahn was another teacher who, while dismissive of him as a mere stand-up comedian, was won over after seeing his performance as a young man in Tennessee Williams' The Night of the Iguana, which was a huge success.

Williams stayed at The Juilliard for another two years before departing without graduating. Again, different stories differ as to why. He may have been evasive about the cause for his leaving a few decades ago. According to other accounts, he left on his own initiative - yet again. However, author Andrea Olmstead claims in her book Juilliard: A History that the school told him to leave, however she did include this in a list of 'blunders that would later humiliate the school'. Indeed, The Juilliard has made a big deal out of its affiliation with Robin Williams, and whatever they thought at the time, they surely were very proud of it. He himself never shed any light on the matter, declaring in 2001 that "he has no degrees from any colleges yet." (Juilliard later bestowed an honorary degree on him.) However, it appears that The Juilliard badly underestimated him, viewing him as a humorist rather than an actor, and therefore missed the depths below.

Gerald Freedman, dean emeritus of the School of Drama at the North Carolina School of the Arts in downtown Winston-Salem, was Williams' Julliard teacher, and an interview he conducted after Robin's death may shed more insight on the matter. 'This is heartbreaking... He was a creative genius... 'I was his Juilliard teacher,' he told Time Warner Cable News. 'He wasn't a good fit for a conservative, traditional training regimen, but we recognized his talent and he was a good sport about it. Nobody was surprised when he dropped out of school before graduating and became what he became. I'm very sad we had to lose him in this way. He had a lot to say about the world in which we live. Maybe it all got to him. 'I'm not sure.'

Are you a good sport? This would imply that his departure was not wholly of his own volition, but rather the result of his failure to control his own sense of anarchy, and that the fact that he had to transform every performance into a humorous turn was, once again, an indication of a genuine desire within him. He had previously claimed to have a 'Love Me' condition, and now it was expressing itself again.

Williams' temperament, according to Robert M. Beseda, was simply unsuited to rigorous learning. 'He was a brilliant mimic - he could impersonate all the teachers, which maybe they didn't like,' he told News Piedmont. Many students who went on to study at The Juilliard acknowledged Robin Williams as one of their inspirations and one of the reasons they were driven to act, which was undoubtedly one of life's ironies. It also hinted that he might be a little rash when confronting authority officials. And the authorities were not pleased.

A third account of events has subsequently surfaced - admittedly a much later one and one that may resemble some face-saving on The Juilliard's part. It has been reported that none other than John Houseman urged Williams to depart because there was nothing else The Juilliard could teach him and he should start obtaining his comedy certification right immediately. This isn't exactly accurate; The Juilliard is the type of place that always believes it can educate people more. Williams, on the other hand, stayed deafeningly silent. Clearly, he never felt compelled to provide his side of the tale, preferring to let it be.

Another perspective came from actor James Marsters, who played Spike in the TV series Buffy The Vampire Slayer (1997-2003) and also left The Juilliard early. In 2001, he told Mediatainement Online, "The joke about Juilliard is that the only actors who end up working are the ones who get kicked out." 'Robin Williams, John Hurt - the list goes on and on of those who were told they would never be performers and that they should leave before they became bitter. Juilliard is a highly disciplined acting institution, and if you have your own spirit, they will try to crush it. And, in my opinion, my instincts as an actor are the only thing I have to contribute, which I will not give up. So... it's pretty sweet. I don't want to talk too much about Juilliard except that it was not the right curriculum for me, and we both knew it.'

It wasn't the ideal program for Robin either, but it didn't really matter in the long run. However, he certainly had no ill will because he eventually financed other aspiring students to attend The Juilliard who would not have been able to do so otherwise. Jessica Chastain was one such lucky recipient. In 2011, she told Interview magazine, "I'm the first person in my family to go to college." 'We didn't have much money, and Juilliard is an expensive school. Robin Williams is a very generous Juilliard graduate who awards a scholarship to a student every two years that pays for everything, and I received it. I'm still waiting to meet him.'

She was understandably moved to pay tribute in the aftermath of his passing. 'It was Robin Williams who transformed my life,' she remarked. 'He was a wonderful actor and a wonderful person. He helped me graduate from college by providing a scholarship. His generous spirit will always encourage me to help others as he helped me. He will be sorely missed.'

Of course, in subsequent years, the many institutions where Williams studied were all eager to associate themselves with such a brilliant actor and humorous genius as he was. He even kept in touch with some of them, like James Dunn at College of Marin, and his death came as a huge shock to the institutions and persons involved in his career, with many of them wanting to pay tribute to the master who had left them (and everyone else) behind.

'For the first time his eyes appeared deep set and his face looked worn,' Dunn, who had seen Williams on occasion throughout the years, told MailOnline of their last meeting. 'He had an impish charm about him for as long as I can remember, but it had faded. He always had this aura around him. He was always the centre of female attention. You couldn't help but love him, and it definitely rubbed off on the ladies. He was a womaniser without a doubt, and he always seemed to be able to deal with everything.' (It should be noted that Dunn was referring to the past, not Robin's joyful marriage to his third wife, Susan Schneider.)

'He was a clever person,' he went on to say. 'And, despite his serious heart problems, Robin appeared to be in fantastic form until lately. Other individuals have demons, but Robin was not one of them; I never regarded him as a gloomy person, although other comics do. I believe it is difficult to be hilarious and to draw out the oddities of life. He did a lot of drugs and then got clean. Then he became addicted to alcohol and spent time in recovery. "Well, he lived life," you think, "he was like a moth to a flame - eventually he burned out."

It should be noted that not everyone agrees with Dunn; many people believe that Robin Williams had a very dark side. Even at his most frantic times, there remained an underlying sadness. Naturally, his death had an impact on The Juilliard. Ironically or not, Robin Williams is one of its most famous alumni, the youngster who was thought to be too unique to train as an actor but turned out to be one of the best of all time. It released the following statement.

JUILLIARD SCHOOL STATEMENT ON THE DEATH OF ROBIN WILLIAMS

The death of our outstanding alumnus Robin Williams has deeply devastated the Juilliard community. Robin's talent for humorous improvisation, which emerged early in his Juilliard training, was matched by his deep understanding of the actor's craft and how to connect with his audience in important ways. He was a generous supporter of the School's drama students through the Robin Williams Scholarship, which covered a drama student's tuition each year. As an artist, he combined a distinct blend of traditional actor training and a creative energy to set new standards for performance in film, television, and live theatre. All who were touched by this remarkable guy will miss his loving ways and bright personality.

Chapter 4.

SEVENTIES SENSATION

Williams returned to California after Juilliard, where he would spend the rest of his life. Whatever his previous experiences had been - and his acting dreams were as strong as ever - one thing was certain: he had been endowed with a humorous genius, which he was determined to put to good use. However, in his own words, it arose as a result of his acting not going so well: 'I left school and couldn't get an acting job, so I started attending stand-up comedy clubs,' he explained. 'I've always improvised, and stand-up was a huge comfort for me. It was suddenly just myself and the crowd.' And didn't he make good use of it?

Of course, Robin had some past stand-up experience, but it was now time for him to make it his career. He had already performed in San Francisco, but it was time to go on to the Los Angeles circuit, where he began performing. And, as has been widely reported since then, including by Williams himself, he began on a path of self-destruction including alcohol and narcotics. He was not alone... During this time, he discovered "drugs and happiness," he revealed, adding that he witnessed "the best brains of my time turned to mud."

The 1970s LA comedy club scene produced some of the top artists in the American entertainment industry to this day. It is a testament to Williams' creativity that he stood out among the likes of David Letterman, Andy Kaufman, Jay Leno, Richard Lewis, Sam Kinison, Elayne Boosler, Tom Dreesen, and George Miller, who all emerged about the same period. They were all remarkable performers in their own right. However, Williams went on to outperform everyone. Almost immediately, he created a stir: 'He seemed to be omnipresent back then and was a topic of debate wherever he went,' novelist Merrill Markoe remarked. He was described as a "comedy cyclone." He was the id, ego, and superego all at once in his act.'

Much has been written about Robin's dramatic, completely insane stand-up style, but it defies understanding in some respects, other than to say that the small child who so desperately sought his mother's attention was not so enthusiastically begging for adoration from the entire world. His performances were more than just energetic and frenetic. They appeared hazardous at times, not because of the subject matter (which was frequently quite risqué), but because of what it revealed about the creator's own mental state. Vincent Canby, an American film critic from Chicago like Williams, once stated that the monologues were so powerful that his 'creative process may invert into a complete meltdown' - a pretty prescient assessment, given what transpired at the end was nearly exactly that. Robin attempted to explain it: the flow of thoughts was never-ending, he claimed, since there was always something going on in the world for him to react to. The audience was kept intrigued by free association. And so forth.

Williams acknowledged Jonathan Winters, Peter Sellers, Mike Nichols, Elaine May, and Lenny Bruce as early inspirations on his act. He appreciated their acts because they were not only tremendously humorous, but also extremely intelligent. All were as learned as he was, yet none of them, not even Sellers, who Robin most closely resembled as an actor, were anywhere near as intense.

He was particularly impressed by the work of Jonathan Winters, the improvised comic who appeared in the hit sci-fi comedy TV series Mork & Mindy, who was likewise a bundle of energy with a natural talent for mimicking. Williams' explanation for why he liked him is a fairly accurate summation of his own work. 'That everything is conceivable, and anything is amusing...' He taught me that it can be free-form, that you can simply go in and out of things,' novelist, pundit, and critic Gerald Nachman quotes him as saying. That was true, and to some extent, anyone could do stand-up... But how do you do it well? That required a very unique talent, and it was clear that

Robin was growing it in spades.

He also enjoyed working with Winters. 'It was a thrill,' he stated in a Reddit interview in 2013. 'I believe I remarked at the Academy Awards that it was like dancing with Fred Astaire, but it was even better because being around him, he would perform for anyone. There was no such thing as a small audience. I think I saw him do a cat for a beagle once. And I experienced a similar experience while watching The Tonight Show with my father. Watching and laughing at Jonathan with my father helped us grow a lot closer. "Have you ever undressed in front of a dog?" is my fave Jonathan Winters one-liner. Williams was also a huge fan of Peter Sellers, whom he first heard on the BBC Home Service radio show The Goon Show, which was groundbreaking at the time, and in an interview, he told presenter Michael Parkinson about Sellers' performance in the film Dr. Strangelove, 'It doesn't get any better than that.' Influences included Peter Cook and Dudley Moore, who were at the vanguard of the early 1960s satire boom, as well as another group of erudite and well-educated men. Richard Pryor was another, albeit he, like Robin, succumbed to alcohol and drugs.

In reality, with the probable exceptions of Nichols and May, every single one of the artists Williams cited as early influences was not only incredibly humorous but also extremely wounded. Winters had two major breakdowns and spent time in a psychiatric facility. Peter Cook developed a drinking problem. Dudley Moore battled depression. Peter Sellers was never himself: only happy when performing, he died of a heart attack at the age of fifty-four, leaving behind a bereaved family. Lenny Bruce was a heroin addict who died of an overdose at the age of forty. Richard Pryor, who died at the age of 65 from a heart attack in December 2005, had drink and drug issues that were, if anything, worse than Robin's. It was turning out to be more than a coincidence. Indeed, the majority of the best comedians are wounded - they make people laugh to distract themselves from their own suffering.

So began Williams' career, which was both the best and worst path he could have taken. His energy and exuberance had to find an outlet somewhere, and what better way than to make people laugh? He talked about personal matters, he told broadcaster Michael Parkinson, since it was 'cheaper than treatment' - a salient point, not least because he himself would wind up in therapy for a significant portion of his life. In some ways, this was correct. If there were emotional troubles in his personal life that could make him cry (and there were - Robin was far more quickly driven to tears than anyone realised back then), it must have seemed like a heavenly relief to take those same issues and make people laugh.

At the same time, it was a frenzied existence, not one meant to quiet down a man already on the verge of a breakdown. It was unstable: performances were held at night, and the performer, having given his all, ended on a high note. What are the next steps? At that point, I was on another high, this one chemically induced. Williams later admitted that he never drank or used drugs before a performance, but he did so afterward and frequently played while hungover. He only performed once while high on cocaine, which he claimed made him paranoid; it was a bad combination.

Then there was the fact that he was continually being made aware of other growing talents, as well as being surrounded by all manner of temptation that would be difficult to ignore. In Gerald Nachman's outstanding book, Seriously Funny: The Rebel Comedians of the 1950s and 1960s, he is reported as stating, "It's a brutal field, man." 'They exhaust themselves. It has an effect. Furthermore, there is the lifestyle - partying, drinking, and doing drugs. It's considerably worse when you're on the road. You have to come back down to mellow your ass out before you can perform. They burn out because it is fleeting. They're suddenly hot, and then someone else is. They can become quite bitter at times. They sometimes just give up. They may have a resurrection and then return. They occasionally snap. The pressure builds. You become preoccupied, and then you lose the necessary focus.'

However, not everyone thought Robin's issues were worse than anyone else's. After all, it was the 1970s, and nearly everyone in show business was on drugs. 'Anyone who grew up during that time had those memories,' said Chris Albrecht, CEO of Starz and a close friend of Robin's. 'Robin was not unusual in this regard. The year was 1970.' That is true, but he also had a melancholy streak, an addictive personality, and a weakness that was not apparent when you saw him on stage or, indeed, in private for most people. He had a self-destructive personality that would be exacerbated by drug use.

'Every night was different,' James Dulworth, now a manager at Dangerfield's Comedy Night Club in Manhattan, said CBS News after Williams' death. When Williams arrived on the scene, he was working as a booker at the Comedy Store. And he claimed that Robin's improvisation was more practised than it appeared: 'He developed cards pretty much in his brain for every occasion for every single night,' he said. 'He had those prepared for nearly any situation. Mitzi Shore, Pauly Shore's mother, owned the Comedy Store,' he continued. 'I was working for her at the start, and she tracked [Williams] down in San Francisco and brought him down [to Los Angeles].'

Others who watched him perform at the time describe him as a mad genius. 'He had the audience in fits of laughter,' recalled Mark Breslin, who had engaged Williams to perform at the club he operated in Toronto at the time. He was speaking to CBC News as the new head of the Yuk Yuk's chain of comedy clubs. 'He was doing personalities and accents, as well as strange associations and word games. He made the entire club his stage. He walked around the tables and performed stand-up comedy. He was really incredible.'

People were taken aback by the breadth of his subject matter. He'd be quoting Shakespeare one moment and grabbing his crotch the next to make sure 'Mr Happy' was home (quoting Shakespeare in the character of someone else, such as Jack Nicholson or Marlon Brando, would become a specialty and was put to excellent use in the 1989 film Dead Poets Society). He went all over the place, pretending to be Elmer Fudd and performing rock tunes before launching into a political riff. It was difficult for the audience to become bored or to guess what would happen next. 'Reality! 'What a notion!' he would exclaim, but it was sometimes difficult to tell how well he understood reality.

There was a combination of humour and satire - material that would have been amusing at any time, as well as material that was quite contemporary, reflecting on current events. Was it draining? Williams would continue his stand-up routines well into his television career, leaving the set to amuse another audience, but clearly the passion and intensity had a sinister side. He was relishing in the pleasure of an audience that was wild with laughter on stage, but backstage it was like coming down from a high. It was maybe unavoidable for someone with his personality that this would leave a need that needed to be filled in some way. And it wasn't hard to figure out where it would be.

Even back then, it was clear that he was a tortured soul. He was getting heavily into alcohol and drugs, and the perceptive recognized that this would not end well. 'I'll never forget how sensitive he was,' Dulworth remarked. 'You could see how he may grow depressed. Being him was probably not easy. He couldn't possibly go out there and not be cheerful and energetic. He most likely required some of those "boosters" to maintain his fast-paced, exuberant attitude. To maintain that level of performance, he almost had to use pharmaceuticals. It's nearly like steroids for athletes.' But the truth remained that he was rapidly developing a drinking and drug addiction that he would battle for the rest of his life.

He had many other problems to contend with, but the one that seemed to bring him the greatest personal pain was that he stole other people's property. Most comedians will agree that it is difficult, at the very least, not to be aware of other people's material and to unwittingly recycle it, but with Robin it went much beyond. In 1989, GQ Magazine noted, 'His reputation for grabbing jokes and instantly making them his own is unrivalled, dating back to his meteoric breakthrough in the sitcom Mork & Mindy.' It actually predated that. Some comedians not only accused him of outright stealing jokes, but also hesitated to perform in front of him for fear that their stuff might end up spilling out of his lips.

'When he walks into a room, a lot of comedians don't want to hit the stage,' the artistic coordinator of a major comedy club told Rolling Stone in 1991. I believe Williams has a large cloud over his head and is kept at arm's length from the comedy community.' However, comedienne Whoopi Goldberg defended him. 'They made it sound like Robin was taking away their livelihood,' she added. 'This happens all the time in comics. Someone says a great line, and you remember it and utilise it. "Make my day," everyone was saying, is that theft?'

One of Williams' most famous remarks, 'Cocaine is God's way of warning you, you have too much money,' was uttered to him by a stranger. But it was a charge that bothered him for the rest of his life.

'I'm not sitting here pleading not guilty,' he told Rolling Stone. 'If you watch comedy for eight hours a day, something will register and spill out. And if that happened, I apologised. I'll compensate you for this." But I wasn't going to go fucking grave robbing on purpose. Because if you're on top, they'll look for your a$$. 'Then I became weary of just paying and being the chump,' he continued. "Hey, wait a minute," I said. It isn't true." People accused me of stealing items that were essentially from my own life. "Wait, this is fucking nuts," I said. That didn't work for me. That concerns my mother." 'Many comedy clubs are like Appalachian encounter groups,' he continued. 'Everyone is doing everything else. You can walk into a club and witness fifteen different people chewing each other up. "Hello, you prick," you say. That's all mine. "Hello," I wrote." So there was some professional envy, but not so much that he insisted on standing outside a club before performing so that no one could ever accuse him of stealing their jokes. 'I do it now as a deliberate effort, so no one can fucking blame me. 'I'm not a necrophile,' he admitted to Rolling Stone. 'I don't need to go back and take another shot.' "Oh, God, don't you just hate it about those medic-alert badges." Yes, thank you. I'll take it. That will definitely work. And many people have taken complete mannerisms from me. It's not something I'm upset about. It's a form of flattery. It's fantastic. When it happens the other way around, you should just smile.' It was true - he was to inspire a whole generation of comic book artists. However, this was to be a reoccurring trend that did not make life any simpler.

However, things were looking up on one front. In 1976, Robin was working in a San Francisco pub when he met Valerie Velardi, a Mills College student who was working as a waitress to pay for her education. She was the eldest of four children and the daughter of an Italian contractor from New Haven, Connecticut, on the East Coast. Valerie's parents split when she was twelve, and she took on the role of mother after her biological mother moved away. That could have influenced her desire for Robin. She was learning to be a dance teacher, having missed out on becoming a dancer herself. Robin characterised her to an interviewer, and the two quickly became an item. They moved in together a month later. She married Williams for the first time in 1978, and the couple had a turbulent relationship. But Robin wouldn't be working in a bar for long. The pair relocated to Los Angeles, where he continued to travel the comedy-club circuit, including an appearance at the Comedy Club in 1977 that

49

altered his life. In the crowd was television producer George Schlatter, a highly seasoned and successful business professional. Schlatter, who was born in Birmingham, Alabama, and raised in Webster Groves, Missouri, began singing at the St Louis Municipal Opera as a teenager, where his mother, a violinist, also sang. He attended Pepperdine University in Los Angeles before becoming an agent with MCA Records; after a few years, he became the general manager of Ciro's Nightclub on the Sunset Strip.

He saw Dan Rowan and Dick Martin perform at Ciro's, and coincidentally, he began creating variety shows and specials for television. It didn't take him long to realise the two should go together. Rowan & Martin's Laugh-In (the title was a reference to the various sit-ins and love-is prevalent in sophisticated society at the time) was intended to be a one-off show in 1967. It was so popular that a regular series was created, which ran from 1968 until 1973, replacing The Man From U.N.C.L.E. on Monday nights at 8 p.m. There were gags, sketches, and much more, all based on vaudeville with a dash of satire (the satire craze was in full swing at the time). It was the first television show to showcase music videos, and it was also notable for starting the career of actress Goldie Hawn, among other things.

Schlatter was looking for new talent because the show had been one of the biggest triumphs in television history, and he was thinking of reviving it. And boy, did he come across it that night. 'He [Williams] extended the microphone over the audience and said, "I'm fishing for assholes,"' he said. Schlatter remembered. In order to resurrect the Laugh-In show, he engaged Robin to perform on the NBC special The Great American Laugh-Off in late 1977. Williams' range of knowledge astonished Schlatter, as it did many others: 'He's one of the most well-educated comedians we've ever had,' Schlatter told Variety. 'Part of that was due to the depth of information and expertise he gained at Juilliard.'

Robin was intended to have a five-minute slot, but it was increased to fifteen minutes. And he was the show's undisputed success from the start, shaking hands with a startled lady and exclaiming, 'She touched me like she knows me!' 'I'm selling my clothes to go to Heaven!' It was clear that a rare talent had arrived. The cast was forced to open something resembling stable doors, stick their heads out, and introduce themselves: in Robin's instance, the relevant door was really in the floor, but as he bobbed up to give his name, he emitted amazing energy even in that moment alone. Williams was also in charge of the show's one remark that made it onto the IMDb website: 'Ladies and gentlemen, I'm here tonight to speak with you about the very severe subject of schizophrenia.' He does not! - SHUT UP AND LET HIM TALK!' He was the evening's unquestioned star, a great new talent now appearing on national television.

Joan Rivers, a comedienne and TV host, met him while filming the show, but she wasn't as taken with him as the rest of the cast. She had the impression that he was still auditioning in some respects, that he was so determined to be seen that he never stopped. 'You know how it is: you're suffering, you want to be recognized, and the only way to get noticed is to be the funny boy,' she told New York Magazine in 1993. "We took a photo together, and he never stopped mugging. You wanted to bind him and tell him, "Stop."

Everyone else, on the other hand, was completely won over. But Robin had been striving for years to get to this position. He'd been perfecting his stand-up act, and his commitment to rehearsals was matched to his ability to improvise - considerably more preparation went into the act than most people realised. He was also developing a signature style by this point, one that he would stick with for a while: vividly coloured braces ('suspenders,' as they were known in the States). No one could ever describe him as a sharp dresser, but he understood the value of presentation and establishing a unique appearance that others could associate with him.

In the end, the show didn't quite match the original's success, but it was clear that a major new talent had arisen on the scene. Schlatter signed him up to be a regular cast member in his Laugh-In series of revivals. 'You didn't really need to bother writing for him,' said Merrill Markoe, a humorist. 'He blew through what he did and seized the show when the camera was on.' (Rowan and Martin, meanwhile, were not amused: they were not involved in the resurrection but owned the format to the program, so they sued. In 1980, they won $4.6 million.)

The rate at which Williams rose was astounding, but it would also contribute to his troubles. It takes time for anyone to adjust to being famous, but when it occurs nearly overnight, the pressure may be almost unbearable. For Robin, reality was shifting at an alarming rate. Another motivation to self-medicate started to emerge. Fame brings pressure and continual attention, and he was struggling to deal with both.

There was also an appearance on The Richard Pryor Show, but something much greater was in the works, something that would need him to go to court in order to be released from his Laugh-In contract. He was making $1,500 per hour on Laugh-In and stood to earn $15,000 each episode if the new arrangement went through. In the end, he was able to get out of his contract, marry Valerie, and look forward to a happy future. The wedding was a big deal: the pair married on June 4, 1978, at The Farms Country Club in Wallingford, Connecticut, where Valerie's father Leonard was a member. Both were delighted about the marriage at first, but the timing was bad because Robin's rapid and dizzying shift in status meant that he was about to enter a crazy stage of his life. He had made a great impact with just one television appearance, and it had caught the attention of some very significant people.

One of the era's greatest comedians was about to become a household name.

Chapter 5.

NANU NANU

Garry Marshall had a problem: he was the writer, director, and producer of Joyful Days, a long-running hit about a joyful family growing up in the 1950s and 1960s. It began in 1974 and was scheduled to end in 1984, but halfway through the run, Marshall attempted to widen its audience. When he asked his son what he wanted to watch, he received an unexpected response.

In 1993, he told New York Magazine, "My 7-year-old son Scott was reluctant to watch Laverne & Shirley or Happy Days or any show I did." "'What do you like?" I inquired. He stated, "I only like space." I informed him, "I don't do space." "Well, you could do it." "How would you do space in Happy Days?" I wondered. And he added, "It could all be a dream." It was the fourth year of the event, and we were looking for good foes for Fonzie. So we created a part for Mork, the extraterrestrial. And Robin was brought in from my sister Penny's acting class by my sister, the casting agent.'

'Williams was the only immigrant to audition for the role,' Marshall subsequently observed. When he entered the room, Garry motioned for him to have a seat, and Robin instantly placed his head on the chair. It was instantly clear that he was the perfect fit for the part: anarchic and slightly insane, you could easily believe he was an alien.'

'My job stopped being about remembering words or moves and started being about not laughing,' recalls Henry Winkler, who played The Fonz and remembers it well. 'But Robin was so shy that it was difficult for him to talk. He asked me the following question: "After a day of this, how do you perform at the Comedy Store?" I said to him, "After this, you really don't have the energy to perform at night." '

The Season Five episode 'My Favourite Orkan' (a reference to another TV show, My Favourite Martian) aired in February 1978 to rave reviews. It was admittedly a tad far-fetched: it involved an extraterrestrial from the planet Ork, Mork, visiting Earth and attempting to take Richie Cunningham (Ron Howard) as a human specimen. Richie is saved by The Fonz, and it is then revealed that Richie has been dreaming... to begin with. When everyone involved enjoyed it, the finale was rewritten to depict Mork deleting everyone's memory instead. 'We answered, "No, it's not a dream; it's real," Marshall said. It's a new series!"'

It most certainly was. Mork & Mindy, the show that would almost instantly make Robin Williams a household celebrity, was born. Mork (who was developed in a test tube and drinks with his finger) was dispatched to Earth by Orson in a small, egg-shaped spaceship to watch humanity. Orson despised him because comedy is not permitted on Ork. When he arrives on Earth - he lands up in Boulder, Colorado, which would eventually become the location of Robin's tributes - he is dressed in a suit but puts it on backwards. He then meets Mindy (Pam Dawber), who has recently broken up with her boyfriend, and believes him to be a priest until he reveals his true identity. She vows to protect his secret and to assist him in his studies of Earth. Mork informs her about his earlier visit to Earth, and The Fonz arranges for him to date Laverne De Fazio (from Laverne & Shirley, one of several crossovers between Mork & Mindy and other television shows - Henry Winkler and Penny Marshall starred).

Mork moves in with Mindy, much to the disgust of her father Fred (albeit her grandmother Cora, with whom she works at Fred's music business, adores him), but the local sheriff, Deputy Tilwick, who believes Mork is insane, attempts to evict him. Mork agrees to depart in the second episode, but his preparations are derailed when he becomes bezurb (drunk) on ginger beer and also discloses to Fred that he is an alien. Mork has a crisis of conscience after missing a date with Mindy in the third episode, and while seeking for a place to stay, he meets the eccentric Exidor, about whom more below. In the following episode, Mindy advises Mork that he needs to experience love in order to understand what it means to be human - yet this plainly leads to a 'will they?/won't they?' issue. Mork believes her and falls in love with a mannequin named Dolly. It was evident why Robin was perfect for the part: a childlike innocence was required to pull this one off. However, this is the episode in which Mork and Mindy kiss, and the future is rather obvious.

The following episode, which features a second kiss between them, introduces the character of Susan (more on her later), who attempts to flee with Mork in retaliation for Mindy stealing her boyfriend in high school. But she is unsuccessful. After a newspaper reporter arrives hunting for evidence of alien life, Fred saves Mork's life. Mork then pretends to predict the weather, prompting Mindy to urge him not to lie ('splinking'), following which he resurrects the vile landlord Arnold (more on that later.) Mork is imprisoned with Exidor in the following episode after falling for a sob story - somewhat awkwardly for the current spectator, Exidor worships O.J. Simpson. Mindy is briefly reunited with her ex-fiancé, while Mork uses his Orkan age machine to shrink himself to the age of three (this gadget was perfect for Williams' talents and also enabled numerous other plot twists). Mork then saves Mindy from an unwanted suitor who is enraged and must be dealt with, after which he uses his age machine to become an older friend of Cora's, to whom he also discloses his true character.

Next, Mork discovers the actual meaning of Christmas and educates everyone else about it, after inviting the incomprehensible Susan to spend it with them because she has no one else (hints of Robin's future emotive roles there), and then mistaking a Russian immigrant for an extraterrestrial. Franklin, an obnoxious new neighbour, moves in, and Mork performs a wedding ceremony for two pals. Exidor returns, intent on becoming Emperor of Earth, and allows the couple to use his summer home, but havoc ensues. Mork is threatened with a transfer, Sally arrives with a newborn son, whom Mork adores so much that he buys a baby of his own, and finally, in a critically acclaimed episode, Mork shuts down his emotions after a nightmare. Mindy kisses him to relieve the emotions that Mork is unable to contain. It was once again the ideal comedy vehicle for Williams.

Mork and Mr Bickley travel to a singles bar, where they encounter girls who turn out to be robbers. Mr Bickley then turns burglar, stealing Mork's ageing machine and changing his age from a baby to middle age. Mork tries to find work, but his 'birthday' creates a potentially fatal ailment (he must recharge himself with an egg-like 'gleek'), and he loses Mindy's job as a result. When he discovers this, he tells Orson that he wishes he hadn't come to Earth, but Orson shows him what would have happened if he hadn't: Mindy would have married gambling addict Cliff, Fred would have gone on a short-term relationship, Cora would have lived with Mindy, and the music shop would have been sold. The episode was titled 'It's A Wonderful Mork,' after the 1946 Christmas fantasy film It's A Wonderful Life. Exidor returns as a reincarnation of Julius Caesar in the season's last episode, the twenty-fifth, and Mork adopts a caterpillar named Bob as a pet. As a result, the series came to an end.

There could hardly have been a better vehicle for Williams' abilities. He improvised a large portion of his role and rose to fame virtually overnight. Indeed, he improvised so extensively that gaps in the script were left to allow him to write his own monologue. Pam Dawber, his co-star, found it difficult since she had to stop herself from laughing while she watched. The audience clearly thought the whole affair was hilarious: the show was a huge smash, with 60 million viewers tuning in on a regular basis. Robin was quickly signed to a five-year, $3 million contract by Paramount. Williams came from a wealthy family in any case, but for the first time, he appeared to be truly wealthy.

The Mork & Mindy TV show quickly became popular. People began greeting each other with the phrase 'Nanu nanu,' accompanied by a Vulcan salute a la Mr Spock. The Orkan profanity shazbot', as well as Mork's version of OK, entered the language. The series eventually surpassed Happy Days in the ratings. Those were exciting times. Robin and Valerie relocated to a canyon home, and Robin purchased a silver BMW; they began to collect animals. But he was also starting to party hard, and after a day on set, he was either out socialising or performing stand-up comedy, neither of which is a prescription for domestic bliss. It didn't help that Valerie wasn't enjoying herself, which meant Robin was frequently out on his own. He still wore Hawaiian shirts and baggy pants, but the multi-colored braces had to go since they made him too identifiable. His life was being encroached upon by fame. He was linked to model Molly Madden, while Valerie was photographed alone in Italy. On the good side, he began conducting charitable work for organisations such as the Human Dolphin Foundation, which he would continue to do for the remainder of his life.

However, things changed in the show's second season, and it undoubtedly suffered as a result. The emphasis shifted from Mork's attempts to comprehend Earth to his relationship with Mindy, and a younger audience was targeted in an attempt to highlight social concerns rather than simply enjoy the comedy, with Fred and Cora losing their regular roles, though they did return in subsequent episodes. A number of new characters were introduced. The show was changed into a variety of various time slots, which was a mistake, and the crowd began to dwindle.

'At first, it was disheartening because I took it personally, thinking, "Oh, God! "I'm not funny anymore," Williams said to New York Magazine in 1981. 'At long last, I recognized it was a combination of other factors. They were messing with the timetable, switching the time slot every other night. And when we started doing all those sexploitation shows - created particularly to have tiny girls running around in tight costumes and me dressed in drag - parents were upset. Many people who used to watch with their children were turned off by this. Also, some people thought we were being too preachy when it came to topics like euthanasia; we had that one episode with the robot being unplugged.' It was a far cry from the joyous mayhem of the beginning.

There were also growing rumours regarding Robin's personal life, with his name now openly associated with a number of other women. He had to make a concerted effort to calm himself. 'It wasn't the work that depleted me, it was the social life,' he told People Magazine in 1979. 'I was on the verge of collapse. I became so agitated that I scared myself. There was no time to rest, no time to go home and yell "Screw you" to a wall. I was starting to feel like I was going through the ceiling. You must reply "No" or you will go slowly, bozo.'

Meanwhile, Valerie was putting in more effort as well: she had accepted that she was now married to a famous actor and was attempting to play the game, attending industry events with him and being an industry wife, as well as working as an ad hoc dance teacher.

But the show was in trouble. More attempts were made to boost the ratings, and Mork and Mindy married in the fourth season. Mork laid an egg, and they produced a child, Mearth, played by Jonathan Winters (Orkans age backwards). But the magic had worn off, and the show was cancelled in 1982. Ninety-one episodes had been filmed in total. The event taught Williams a valuable lesson that he will never forget: don't be complacent. In a 2009 interview, he told People, "I found out the show was cancelled by reading it in Variety." 'That's like reading your own obituary in Hollywood:

"You're dead, good luck!" It was all a little unfortunate for a man prone to such personal uneasiness.

Apart from Mork and Mindy, the series produced a slew of beloved characters. Both tetchy old Fred (Conrad Janis) and freethinking Cora (Elizabeth Kerr) had a large fan following, and it was a terrible error to lower their characters in retrospect. Franklin Delano Bickley (Tom Poston) lived next door, and Mearth (Jonathan Winters) was their enormous, ancient child. The New York Delicatessen was co-owned by siblings Remo and Jean Davinci (Jay Thomas and Gina Hecht). Mindy's conservative, ambitious relative was Nelson Flavor (Jim Staahl). Then there was Mork's superior, the patient Orson (voiced by Ralph James).

Other recurrent characters with their own roles on the show were also present. Susan Taylor (Morgan Fairchild) is Mindy's snobbish high school classmate. Exidor (Robert Donner) is a prophet who sees Mork for what he is, as well as the leader of a cult that no one else sees. Mr Sternhagen (Foster Brooks) takes over as Mindy's boss at the local TV station, and Todd Norman Taylor (TNT) (Bill Kirchenbauer) is a womanising jock who teaches Mork to drive. In the first series, Eugene (Jeffrey Jacquet) is a ten-year-old boy who meets Mork; Billy (Corey Feldman) is a daycare centre child. The somewhat unfortunate (at least to a British audience!) Fred's music store is owned by Arnold Wanker (Logan Ramsey).

Interestingly, for something that began as such a frivolous bit of entertainment, Mork & Mindy hinted at several factors that could affect Williams' life. He was a highly talented actor, and even the most cynical critics recognized it, but what he excelled at above and beyond anything else was comedy, particularly improvisational comedy. However, he was frequently chastised for being overly emotional at times, and he sacrificed his true talent for something that could be a touch cloying. And that is exactly what happened with Mork & Mindy: the show began as outrageously hilarious but evolved into a program that attempted to comment on current events. This did not work, and the audience disliked it. And, while it would be simple to point the finger at the producers, Robin was also involved in the decision-making process.

This was driven home in a self-indulgent episode ('Mork Meets Robin Williams') from 1981. Mindy purchases a CD by the comedian Robin Williams. When she returns home, she realises he is a carbon copy of Mork. When Mork tunes into Orson, Robin enters and questions the nature of immense stardom, telling him, 'Being a star is a twenty-four hour job and you can't leave your face at the office... some of them can't take it.' He then identifies some of those who were destroyed by fame's pressures: Elvis Presley, Marilyn Monroe, Jimi Hendrix, John Lennon... Given that this episode aired only two months after John Lennon's death, the message was clear: fame can be lethal. It was an uncanny foreshadowing of Williams' own fate, not to mention an indication of his mental state, but it was having his cake and eating it. It wasn't funny, and it wasn't what the audience expected.

It did, however, provide some insight into what was going on behind the scenes. Williams had gone from virtual unknown to one of the world's most famous men in a matter of years, and this was certain to take its toll. It would have been difficult to cope with even the most balanced and steady of creatures, and he was neither. Furthermore, he despised being so closely linked with his extraterrestrial creation: when he went out to play live at nightclubs, which he still did (often after a day's filming), the audience would yell, 'Do Mork!' But Robin refused to do Mork.

Always prone to self-destruction, the crisis had now arrived. Williams, along with his friend and fellow comic John Belushi, was deeply into drugs and alcohol, which was wreaking havoc on his life. Women began to flock to him now that he was famous and becoming increasingly wealthy. He wasn't always turning them down, despite being frequently inebriated and/or high. Of course, this had to have a negative impact on his marriage, and it did. Behind the scenes, things were becoming increasingly tense.

Valerie appeared to be coping at first. She was determined to battle for her man. 'Look, I'm a Goddard College product,' she told Rolling Stone in an incredibly revealing interview in 1982, hinting at far more turbulence in the background. 'Have you heard of it? And it's taught me that you can guide people; that you can make yourself interesting and significant enough in your lover's life that he'll always come back to you if you just keep growing along with it. If you simply become a part of their rhythm and offer them a lot of freedom, you will be a part of their growth rather than dragging them away from what is titillating and thrilling. Let's face it: Robin is a stimulant addict.'

He was far more so than anyone had realised. Not only was the situation becoming unsustainable, but it was also becoming increasingly unpleasant to live with. But Valerie was putting on a brave face for the time being. Asked about other women, she answered, 'That implies no, in a circumstance like that - it's a hard one, because I could be misquoted horrifically. The fact is, it was never a single woman. There were a lot of women, and I'm not sure he had anything intimate to do with all of them. The majority of it was simply hanging out. He adores women and enjoys spending time with them. I have this letter from a woman who was spotted with Robin about town. They were supposed to be having a heated, um, affair, and I met her and she was wonderful. They simply desired to socialise. I can't prevent him from dining with a woman he likes. That's none of my concern, just as I wouldn't want him to prevent me from hanging out with anyone I wanted to. What kind of world is this if he can't have female friends and I can't have male friends, if you have to constantly expect the worst every time someone finds someone else to improve their lives in some way?'

What about enviousness? 'I become envious. 'I'd only be envious if I thought someone was stealing my position,' she continued. 'And it's always been evident that we have it. It's us. It doesn't sit right, but in extreme situations like ours, if you don't make the appropriate adjustments, you could lose valuable items. That's not to suggest we have carte blanche to wreck everything in our path. It's just the freedom to feel like we're free individuals rather than married and bound in. You can't go out tonight because I know so and so is there, and she's hot and attractive, and I'm scared you'll get connected with her. He'll never become involved with anyone without my knowledge. And the other option is ineffective. You can't keep someone in. They dislike you, and you become uninteresting and unappealing. If I had divorced him too soon, I would have lost the most precious thing in my life, and it would have limited our experience together, which is far more valuable than anything he can buy off the street.'

Valerie's fortitude was remarkable, but it was never going to work. Robin was essentially doing what he wanted and agitating her so badly that she would storm out, take herself out for a few days of hiking, sometimes go on vacation, and only return when she had cooled down. Her view at the time was that, while Robin was misbehaving, the other women didn't matter to him. After all, she was his wife. While this was true, it was becoming increasingly impossible to overlook the fact that her husband's success had turned him into a drug-abusing womaniser. Things were about to get much messier, but she was determined to keep things going for the time being.

Who could blame her? In other ways, her life had improved as well: being married to a huge star came with its own set of pressures, but the pair was also beginning to enjoy a very decent quality of living. It wasn't only the nicest tables at the best restaurants; these days, everyone wanted to meet Robin. He was talked about everywhere, and his celebrity opened doors that most of us do not have. And, of course, when he was on form, Robin was fantastic company. Valerie, obviously, desired for the relationship to succeed.

By now Robin had bought a property in Topanga Canyon and another car: an old Land Rover - 'I can't deal with new cars. I like an automobile that is like me in that you never know what will come next.' He wasn't interested in material things for their own sake, even if the money was rolling in rapidly by this point.

What he did want was a Hollywood career, and in 1980, he made his formal film debut in Popeye, which was largely regarded as a flop, with Shelley Duvall co-starring as Olive Oyl. (He also appeared in the 1977 picture Can I Do It 'Til I Need Glasses. Fortunately, this was forgotten and is nearly never addressed in Williams' work. It sank without a trace, and rightly so.) There were high hopes for his latest production, not least because it was directed by Robert Altman and produced by Robert Evans (the original leads were Dustin Hoffman and Lily Tomlin), but the musical comedy was a critical flop (though not a commercial one, grossing more than twice its $30 million budget at the box office).

One issue was the plot, which was confused and disjointed. Not all of the critics despised it, but some did. 'With this shockingly monotonous musical, E.C. Segar's beloved sailorman aboard a sinking ship,' said respected reviewer Leonard Maltin in his movie guide. 'With an insipid script, crowded staging, and some purported songs, a game cast does its best. Instead, watch a few hours of Max Fleischer cartoons; you'll be much happier.' The only part of the film that earned positive feedback was Harry Nilsson's music. However, most people believed the rest of it was a shambles.

It was a poor debut for someone who had so much riding on it, but Robin took it in stride. He still had several seasons of Mork & Mindy left, and producers and directors were lining up to work with him.

While some flops have ended cinematic careers prematurely, this was not the case here. Williams was riding a tide of adoration as Hollywood savoured the gifted newcomer, and only his inner circle was aware that he was paying a horrible price. His drug usage was out of control, and his marriage was still suffering because, intoxicated by everything that came his way, he acted like a child let loose in a candy store when it came to women. Valerie could only stare in misery.

It wasn't just his wealth and celebrity that made him appealing. Robin actually enjoyed ladies but was an awful flirt. Furthermore, his wit and vivacity were extremely appealing in and of themselves, let alone in someone who was quickly becoming such a tremendous star. Valerie persisted, and the marriage was to survive for a while longer, but the couple's pleasant facade was becoming increasingly difficult to maintain. There were squabbles and sadness, and while Valerie felt Robin had turned a corner, the truth was that he hadn't. He was quickly becoming recognized as a drug-addicted womaniser, and it would take a catastrophe to get him to face the fact that his demons were out of control.

Chapter 6.

THE WORLD ACCORDING TO ROBIN

By the early 1980s, Williams knew exactly what he intended to do: break into the mainstream of acting. After all, he had trained at The Juilliard as an actor, not a stand-up comedian, and if they hadn't recognized his potential there, it was their fault. And, while Popeye had been a flop, there were plenty of other ideas in the works. But what he did next surprised everyone. John Irving's fourth novel, The World According to Garp (1982), was a best-seller and winner of the National Book Award for Fiction. It was to be made into a film, which would also star John Lithgow in a lead role. (Lithgow went on to star in the TV series 3rd Rock From The Sun [1996-2001], as another extraterrestrial in a suburban-set comedy that owes a lot to Mork & Mindy.) Jenny Fields (Glenn Close, who was still relatively unknown at the time - this was her feature film debut) is a nurse during WWII who becomes pregnant through a dying soldier known only as Garp. She eventually has a son.

Garp becomes a renowned writer, married to Helen Holm (Mary Beth Hurt), with whom he has two children, Duncan and Walt, while Jenny becomes a feminist icon. Helen becomes engaged with one of her students, which Garp discovers, and he collides with his wife's lover's car while she performs a sex act on him. Walt is killed in the collision, and Duncan is injured in one eye. Despite this, the couple reconciles and has a second child, Jenny.

The original Jenny now runs a transgender center, and it is while visiting the center that Garp learns about Ellen James, a girl who was gang-raped and then had her tongue removed so she could not identify her perpetrators. Some of the ladies at Jenny's centre are 'Ellen Jamesians,' or women who cut out their own tongues in solidarity. Garp is appalled by the practice and discovers that the Jamesians have received a letter from Ellen James herself pleading with them to stop, but they have voted to continue.

Jenny is the target of death threats, as is Garp after he writes a book on Ellen James. An anti-feminist extremist shoots and kills Jenny. The women at the centre are holding a memorial for her, but all men are barred from attending. Garp is hidden inside the memorial dressed as a woman, but his identity is discovered and he is in danger from the women, one of whom guides him out and turns out to be Ellen James. He, too, is shot, and as he is being taken away in an air ambulance, he has one last recollection of his mother throwing him into the air as a child.

It wasn't Mork and Mindy, nor was it Popeye. This was a solid, meaty dramatic character that required an actor of some skill and aptitude to take on, and considering that Williams was known almost completely for his role as Mork and his stand-up comedy, the world of show business was taken aback when word of the casting leaked out.

'A lot of people felt I was insane to cast Robin,' said director George Roy Hill (Butch Cassidy & The Sundance Kid/The Sting) in an interview with New York Magazine before the film's release. 'However, you make these choices automatically. I'd watched him in the role of Popeye and couldn't comprehend a word he said. I'd seen him before as Mork and had no idea who he was. I assumed he was just a stand-up comedian. However, upon meeting him, I felt he possessed an important sense of decency. Garp is an aggressive character, but his underlying decency is important, and I believed Robin was the type of actor who could deliver that. I hope I'm correct.'

In reality, he was among the first in Hollywood to recognize that Robin Williams was far more than the funny he had previously been known as. He was a brilliantly talented actor with the depth and emotional understanding to play a more serious part. The World

According To Garp was promoted as a comedic drama, despite the fact that it dealt with incredibly serious subjects and was thus likely to be controversial.

'Robin is a phenomenal talent,' stated George Roy Hill. 'He's an actor, a real actor, not just a comedian cast in an acting role. If he puts his mind to it, he can go the entire distance. He's one of the brightest persons I've ever met, in my opinion. He has a fantastic mind, and while he is not an intellectual, he may become one in the future. He's quick, instinctive, funny, and kind, and he's one of the few comedians I've encountered who, while "on" most of the time, isn't aggressively "on." Garp isn't a funny character. He is a serious figure, yet there is comedy, the most of which is based on fact. Robin had to age from 18 to 34 in the picture. He is, in reality, 29, but he has always had an elderly face. I've seen images of him when he was 18 or 19, and he appears older, so he's convincing when he has to act that age.'

Regardless, it was to be a learning experience. Williams had to learn how to regulate himself: his stand-up comedy relied on a rapid-fire delivery, as did his portrayal of the extraterrestrial Mork - in fact, his ability to talk so quickly was one of the many factors that qualified him for the role. George Roy Hill was aware of this. 'Robin had a bad habit that we had to break,' he explained. 'He has a tendency to deliver too quickly - it took me a long time to bring him down to a playing speed since his mind works so quickly. I think I've slowed him down enough, but it could just be that I'm growing used to him.'

It was a learning lesson for Robin as well, and not just in terms of slowing down his delivery. This was a far cry from the type of material he was used to: a demanding dramatic role that would not be simple to pull off. 'The main issue is getting all the varied ages to fit together,' he said to New York Magazine in 1981. 'I have to make all of those stages of life and relationships plausible. I've had to dive deep within myself to consider both sad and good things. There are some vibrant sequences with youngsters, as well as a lot of death and dealing with loss. The scenes with my wife in the film are quite personal, with no pretension. I need to be direct and upfront.'

He also displayed genuine insecurity, the first public indication of a considerably more vulnerable nature than had previously been shown. At that point in his life, Williams was still seen as a clown: a tremendously accomplished clown, to be sure, but a clown nonetheless. No one knew the depths of his sadness, the lonesome side, the aching vacuum within that drink, drugs, and comedy were all being used to kill - at least no one in public. Those who knew Robin well knew that he wasn't always as straightforward as he appeared.

'I haven't seen the rushes because I'm worried they'll jar me,' he acknowledged. 'I don't think I'll see myself until the final cut. It's as if you're drowning or fleeing for your life. I lack perspective. It's not like humour or outright farce, where I can trust my senses. It's all uncharted territory. It's like being in battle. After one day of shooting, I thought to myself, "God, I died." Even though it was only a single moment, I was overcome with emotion and sobbed for several hours afterwards. When I see the finished product, I'll look back and say, "I did that." I'll be pleased. I'm proud now, but I can't say it since it's not over. It's a risk. It's terrifying, truly odd, because every time you try anything completely new, you immediately think, "Oh, no. It's all over now. I'll be selling the National Enquirer door to door starting now."'

Of course, many actors have that dreadful sensation of fear that one day they will be discovered and forced to return to their previous life. However, in Robin's situation, this was heightened by the fact that everything had transpired so quickly. It nearly didn't matter that Mork & Mindy was rapidly losing viewers and would soon be cancelled. He'd made it to the big time, but like so many others, he couldn't perceive the power of his own position. He couldn't see clearly in the midst of the whirlwind that was now his life that he was now so sought after that a successful career was pretty much guaranteed from then on.

'I'm astonished and in shock sometimes,' he admitted to New York Magazine when questioned about his celebrity. 'Sometimes I feel like I'm going back to square one. I go through stages of being afraid. I can't deal with them because they're crippling. I need to attempt new things, like Garp, and challenge myself. You know, the next opportunity. Because my greatest worry is becoming mediocre, simply sliding back into the same old rut and producing the same old stuff without discovering anything new. That applies to life as well - simply trying not to get trapped, this fear of slipping back, sinking back into myself.'

But, for the time being, his relationship with Valerie was stable. For Robin, slowing his delivery meant calming down the frantic speed of his life and appreciating his wife and marriage. After all, Valerie knew him before he became famous, and one key dilemma for many of the wealthy and famous is whether their friends and lovers prefer them because of their status or because of who they truly are. Valerie, who had married Robin when he was a complete unknown, was one of the few individuals with whom he could truly be himself.

'She should definitely return and teach,' he told New York Magazine. 'She has a strong sense of pride in not being known as Mrs. Robin Williams.'There were no managers or press personnel at first, just the two of us. She was significant simply by being present, coming to clubs with me, and hanging out with me. We've now moved on to the next stage. It's all quite emotional. It's great to come home to someone who recognizes you. I can sit without saying anything. I occasionally pass out. I wrestled for thirteen hours the other day. When I returned, I couldn't say anything. I'm not required to entertain or do anything. She is aware. I adore her to pieces. When I gaze at her, I feel really serene. We've gone through some weird stuff, wild and woolly times. It's now like, "Look - land!" Garp has sparked something in me. Simple things now make me happy. I enjoy lengthy walks, being outside, and simply doing stuff with friends more than I used to. It's fantastic. Previously, I was expected to go out and party, perform, and always be "on." Now I'm willing to sit back and listen.'

For the time being, at least... there was more trauma to come.

The World According To Garp was released in July 1982, and for critics, Williams was a revelation. They did not necessarily give the film totally great reviews, not least because many people did not seem to enjoy either the strange plot or the novel on which it was based, but they were impressed by what they had seen.

'Robin Williams has the acting chops to win an Oscar,' stated Juicy Cerebellum's Alex Sandell. In the Mountain Xpress, Ken Hanke remarked, "Good effort, sometimes nearly great."

'The World According to Garp 'was adapted for the film by Steve Tesich, and George Roy Hill directed,' said Frederic and Mary Ann Brussart in Spirituality and Practice. 'Tesich's superb humanism and Hill's healthy respect for life's serio-comic elements make this one of 1982's best films. The performances are all excellent. True to the novel's ethos, the plot forces us to contemplate the uncertainties of love, death, sex, and violence that characterise modern existence.'

'Garp simply does not understand, and for good cause. 'Despite his strange conception and upbringing, he's the eternal Everyman,' commented Q Network Film Desk's James Kendrick. 'All he wants is a good family and to be recognized for something. His suburban life pales in comparison to his mother's feminist retreat, which is populated with tongueless ladies and sexually transformed football stars such as Roberta Muldoon (John Lithgow). Robin Williams may appear to be a weird choice for the part of a typical guy, but he actually performs well in it. He's good at showing his absolute surprise at the bizarre goings-on around him, while Jenny merely stands back and smiles, never once thinking that any of this is odd.'

Meanwhile, Variety was favourable of the picture, albeit not entirely convinced about Robin. 'Garp grows up in a tranquil academic setting, and the grown man in the figure of Robin Williams arrives after only 25 minutes,' it wrote. 'He meets and marries Mary Beth Hurt, raises his family, fitfully pursues his writing while she teaches, has battles with the feminists at his mother's home, and all the while strives to avoid the "undertoad", the unseen, ubiquitous threat which lurks everywhere and strikes without warning. Physically, Williams is fine, but most of the performance is hit-and-miss. Otherwise, casting is superior. Hurt is terrific as Garp's wife. Glenn Close proves a superb choice as Jenny Fields, a woman of almost ethereal simplicity. Best of all, arguably, is John Lithgow as Roberta Muldoon, a former football player, now a transsexual.'

Time Out was also unconvincing. 'Williams is lovable enough as the father whose gifts for raising a family are constantly thwarted by a malevolent fate, and Lithgow gives a dignified performance as a six-and-a-half-foot ex-pro footballer transsexual,' it said. 'However, it's the kind of film that is daring - or dumb - enough to question the meaning of life without having enough arse in its breeches to justify a response.'

Some people noticed Robin's transition from comic to actor. 'Mr. Williams is most endearing to children; he makes a warm, playful father, a man fully at home in a suit of make-believe armour fashioned of welcome mats and garbage-can lids,' observed Janet Maslin in The New York Times. 'Mr. Williams' part is quite demanding, requiring him to mature from an adolescent to a family man, which he finds difficult. His acting is amusing but inconsistent, working better in the clowns, faster sequences than the ones that need him to memorise lines or remain still. Mr. Williams is significantly less compelling when he is not representing Garp through action. He falters when the part does not need movement of some type.'

Some people simply couldn't get into the movie. 'What are we to make of these people and the circumstances in their lives?' wondered Roger Ebert in the Chicago Sun-Times. 'I thought the performance was unusual and engaging (particularly by Williams, Glenn Close as his mother, and John Lithgow as a transsexual). Director George Roy Hill's representation of the events was innovative and consistently engaging to me. But as the movie ended, my initial reaction was not what it should have been. All I could think of was, 'What the heck was it all about?'

'There's no feeling of realism in either the book or the movie,' Pauline Kael said, and the 'mostly faithful adaptation seems little more (and no less) than a castration dream.'

Whatever others thought of it, it demonstrated that Robin Williams could act. Some, like film critic Roger Ebert, believed he was primarily a comedian rather than an actor, but it was evident from then on that his talents ran far deeper than anybody had realised. It was also wonderful timing: Mork & Mindy had just ended, and it was now time to move on to the next act of life.

But something happened three months before the film's release that would have a major impact on Williams' life. His close friend and fellow actor and comic John Belushi died of a drug overdose in March 1982, at the age of thirty-three, after swallowing a speedball (a mixture of cocaine and heroin). He was discovered dead in his Chateau Marmont room on Sunset Boulevard. Williams and fellow actor Robert De Niro both paid him a visit in the early hours of his death. It was a huge shock for everyone involved.

Belushi, like Williams, was a rising celebrity in Hollywood. He, too, had made his name on television - in his case, Saturday Night Live -

and, like Williams, he was a staggeringly talented comic performer, perhaps best remembered for his role in The Blues Brothers (1980), with his great friend Dan Aykroyd, who penned the role of Dr. Peter Venkman in Ghostbusters (1984) with him in mind (the part eventually went to Bill Murray). His rise, like Williams', was fast, and he, too, was learning what a shark pool Hollywood can be. The day before his death, Paramount Pictures pressed him to appear in National Lampoon's The Joy Of Sex (1984), which Aykroyd strongly cautioned against, claiming that they were only utilising Belushi's involvement to get the film made: 'Oh, don't do that, are you kidding me?' he said to his companion. 'Get out, get out!' Come home, it's spring, and something will happen in the summer or fall.' Ghostbusters would almost definitely have been that something, but it was not to be.

Despite the push, Belushi consented to participate in the project. Perhaps it was his inherent disdain for the project, or perhaps it was simply that his drug use had become hopelessly out of control, but he spent his final night with another notorious drug user, Catherine Evelyn Smith, a former back-up singer for The Band, among others, hopping between The Roxy and the Chateau Marmont, with Smith repeatedly injecting him with heroin. He was discovered dead in his bed the next morning. Smith was later caught and charged with first-degree murder; she eventually reduced the conviction to manslaughter and served eighteen months in prison.

Williams had been there earlier, smoking three lines of coke, but he looked repulsed by Smith, whom he described as "creepy." Sadly, it has been reported that he left that night with the words, 'If you ever get up again, call me.' Though it was meant to be a throwaway sentence, it was terrifyingly prescient. Although he was not to fault, Robin would endure great guilt as a result of that night, despite the fact that by that point, it was improbable that anyone could have saved John. Penny Marshall (who directed Robin in Awakenings,

1990) revealed decades later that John was completely incapable of rejecting any kind of temptation, with tragic repercussions. 'You'd walk down the street with him and people would hand him drugs,' he said. 'And then he'd do all of them - be the kind of character he did in skits or Animal House,' she told The Hollywood Reporter after his death thirty years ago. 'I love him, I miss him, and I wish he hadn't been involved with the individuals he was with. People were insane in the '70s and '80s.'

The unexpected death of John Belushi shocked Hollywood and the rest of the globe. Judy, his childhood girlfriend, was over herself with grief. Even though close associates knew Belushi was an addict, he had such a great future ahead of him that no one could comprehend what had transpired.

'What else can I say? 'John was enormously skilled, and I guess you could say he lived life "excessively,"' said music producer Bruce Robb, who had previously worked with him and was also close to Dan Aykroyd. 'I think what happened to John was a wake-up call for a lot of people, including myself.'

And that was devastating for Robin, because John had been a wonderful friend. He had only seen him a few hours before he died, and there were far too many similarities between the two of them for him not to be frightened that the same thing might happen to him. However, it should be noted that his drug use was not on par with John's. In 1991, he told the Los Angeles Times, "It was a strange thing because my managers sent me to this doctor because they said I had this cocaine problem." "How much do you do?" he asked. "A gram every couple of days," I said, and he said, "You don't have a problem." That was before they recognized it was psychologically addictive. Then, at some time, you realise, maybe it is. Physically, I'm not desiring it, but intellectually, I think it's a wonderful idea.'

He was obviously doing enough to realise his habit was out of control, and he was also drinking heavily. It was one of those defining moments in a person's life when anything may happen. Williams, like Belushi, was a young man who had burst onto the scene and had a bright future ahead of him. He might choose to embrace that future, or he could succumb to the dark side, with all of its risks.

There were further motivations for going sober. Robin and Valerie were giving their marriage another shot, so much so that Valerie fell pregnant with Robin's first child a few months after John's death. Robin was wild and irresponsible at the time, but he wasn't stupid, and introducing a baby into the kind of lifestyle he was living was just not on. He realised he needed to quit, so he did. He did not enter rehab at the time, as he would later, but instead, with sheer resolve, he gave up everything, going cold turkey. He was clean for decades after that.

'The Belushi disaster was terrifying,' he subsequently told People. 'His death alarmed a large number of show business individuals. It resulted in a large migration from narcotics. And then there was the impending birth of my child. I realised I couldn't be a father and live that sort of life.'

It seemed a fresh chapter was starting and, to a certain extent, it was. Robin was only at the beginning of an exceptionally successful film career, he had cleaned up his act and he and Valerie had a baby on the way. But he was never fully able to free himself of his demons. Although his marriage was back on track, he would soon find himself embroiled in an affair that resulted in a spectacularly embarrassing court case, making headlines for all the wrong reasons and, despite the fact that he and Valerie worked at it, their marriage was not to last. In one of life's great ironies, Robin Williams, who offered so much joy and laughter to people around him and who was to become such a famous comedian, was never able to make peace with himself.

Chapter 7.

TROUBLED TIMES

London is the capital of England. It was the early 1980s, and one of Hollywood's most promising newcomers was in town. He decided he wanted to do a show in the UK and requested a taxi driver to take him to a comedy club. The taxi driver drove him to The Comedy Store, where regulars Alexei Sayle and Andy de la Tour agreed to Robin Williams' request to play a set, so they sent him on first to warm up the audience before the real pros took the stage. It was a performance that no one in the audience will ever forget. He was supposed to perform fifteen minutes, but that didn't quite work out.

'Forty minutes later, Robin Williams walked off the stage,' de la Tour wrote in Stand-Up or Die. 'The attendance was depleted. They were made fun of. They were not going to laugh at anyone else for at least a year. They were so exhausted and sprawled over the chairs. Williams had given us a comedic performance that was so full of fire and inventiveness that "tour de force" doesn't even come close.'

British viewers seemed to adore him just as much as those on the other side of the Atlantic. He'd already won a Grammy for his 1979 live concert at New York's Copacabana, Reality... What A Concept (the same record Mindy was clutching when she and Mork encountered Robin). Along with his expanding film career, he continued to produce hugely successful television specials such as Off The Wall (1978), An Evening With Robin Williams (1982), and Robin Williams: Live At The Met (1986). He was also quickly becoming a regular on talk shows, first with David Letterman, when he gave another wild performance after becoming renowned as Mork, and then with Johnny Carson. He was to appear on The Late Show with David Letterman fifty times in all, and the host was to become a buddy for the next forty years. Letterman first saw Robin at the LA Comedy Store and recalls thinking, "They're going to have to put a stop to show business because what can happen after this?" He came in like a hurricane,' he said, adding, 'Holy crap, there goes my career in show business.' (In the end, he did OK for himself!)

But he was still determined to advance his cinematic career, and in 1983 he co-starred in another flop, The Survivors, with Walter Matthau. Michael Ritchie has returned to putting whoopee cushions beneath the buttocks of arrogant gurus with his latest social-message comedy, The Survivors, starring Robin Williams and Walter Matthau. 'Rough noises are made, but the laughter is weak and scattered,' noted James Wolcott in Texas Monthly. The great picture success he desired remained elusive.

Robin's first child, Zachary Pym 'Zak' Williams, was born in 1983. Soon after, another film, Moscow on the Hudson (1984), was released, about a Russian musician who defected to New York. It wasn't a huge smash, but it received great reviews and contributed to the developing idea that Robin Williams was a force to be reckoned with.

'Halfway through The World According to Garp, I began to think Robin Williams would require weights in his shoes to keep from floating in the air - he was that insubstantial,' said David Denby in a glowing review for New York Magazine. 'But this time, Williams is grounded; he has a real character to play, and he's extremely sympathetic. He's a diminutive, virtually inconspicuous figure in the Moscow scenes, hugging himself against the cold and grimacing at the sight of a three-hour waiting line for toilet paper.'

Williams, who had recently become sober, was now a family man with a small boy. In an effort to keep clean, he was heavily into cycling, which would prove to be a life-long hobby; only the latest sport that Robin grew interested in. Previously a runner, the activity was beginning to wear on his body, so he discovered cycling to be more relaxing. He managed to stay sober for over two decades before succumbing to relapse. Even so, those devils would not leave him alone for long. Just when he appeared to be cooling down, there was another crisis in his personal life, this time involving a woman who would end up bringing him to court. Robin encountered Michelle Tish Carter, a cocktail server (much like Valerie when he met her), while performing at Improv, a LA comedy club. The two started an affair, although this one lasted a little longer than some of the others before it went tragically wrong.

Michelle sued Robin for $6.2 million in 1986, claiming he gave her herpes without telling her he was afflicted. It was an ugly and embarrassing case, nicknamed 'Financial Attraction' by Williams' lawyers (Fatal Attraction, another story of an initial encounter that goes tragically wrong, had recently come out), and one that reflected poorly on all parties involved. Robin never admitted or denied having the virus, and the lawsuit was eventually settled out of court. He and Valerie separated two years later, but there was another scandal involved as well.

The character of this trial was not unusual at the time. It was the 1980s, when herpes and AIDS were dominating the news, and a lot of sexually active adults were scared of both. Debates had erupted over how much information you should offer your new sexual partner, and both Robin and Michelle were compelled to declare publicly that they had neither asked the other if they had a communicable sexual disease. Robin's lawyer, Philip Ryan, stated that in this case, a person who does not ask for or insist on condoms should be assumed to have taken the risk. Otherwise, he claims, these cases will 'create a judicial ménage à trois,' opening the judiciary to "any forlorn lover whose affair has come to an unexpected end."

Robin himself kept a respectful silence about the virus, but he couldn't help but mention current turbulence in his performance. 'And, as we all know, there's THAT OTHER THING out there,' he said to one of the audience members. 'Which means we all need to employ some condom wisdom. Do you understand what a condom is? The love bathing cap!'A prophylactic, from the Latin prophylactorum, which means unusual party favours. I know you despise putting it on. You don't want to suggest, "Let's stop and put on a balloon."' The piece elicited a great laugh.

One would wonder why, after publicly admitting a certain neediness and basing his entire career on the words "love me," Robin acted so brutally towards a wife who did, in fact, love him and had now given him a son. However, there is no simple answer to this. All that can be said is that Williams was not stable, even after giving up alcohol and narcotics. His crazy side fueled his comedy, but it was also the source of his inability to find serenity. While even his most ardent supporters would struggle to justify his actions, the difficulty was that the harm had already been done. The man who craved love was publicly hurting the lady who gave it to him.

As divorce became unavoidable, the project resumed, this time with a film version of Saul Bellow's novel Seize the Day (1986). Again, it performed admirably but failed to set the world on fire. 'For the most part, Robin Williams is up to it,' observed John Leonard in New York Magazine. 'His tense comedic energy reverses; gazing within, it corrodes rather than tickles. He's all suffering, no smiling, smoking smokes and popping drugs. It's a claustrophobic performance, which is appropriate. His despair and desperation close in on us. And what exactly are his transgressions? Disappointment to his father? Is he going to change his name? Are you going to Hollywood? Do you desire love? Not feeling like you belong? It's no surprise that Williams can't create a cry that reconciles us to the idea of death.'

Robin co-hosted the first Comic Relief in the United States with Whoopi Goldberg and Billy Crystal in 1985, a charity to help the homeless that was based on the UK model and raised upwards of $50 million, and in 1987 he went into therapy ('open-heart surgery in instalments,' he quipped), which he credited with finally giving him the success he craved. Nobody could have expected that - a film about a disc jockey in a war zone? - but his enormous comedic abilities as an actor and a stand-up all came into play with Good Morning, Vietnam (1987).

The plot, loosely based on the experiences of AFRS radio DJ Adrian Cronauer, may have been spun with Robin in mind, since it played wonderfully to his unique talents, as it did in the first series of Mork & Mindy. Cronauer moved to Saigon in 1965 to work for the Armed Forces Radio Service. His reckless demeanour immediately irritates his superiors, notably Sergeant Major Philip Dickerson (J.T. Walsh). Others, on the other hand, enjoy him and his presentation, which is a blend of humour and rock 'n' roll. Williams, like Mork and Mindy, was encouraged to improvise.

Cronauer meets Trinh (Chintara Sukapatana), a young Vietnamese girl, and follows her to an English class that he takes over. He then meets her brother Tuan and takes him to a GI bar. A brawl breaks out. Cronauer is chastised, but business as usual resumes until Tuan drags him out of a pub minutes before it is destroyed by a bomb, which Cronauer reports against orders not to. He is suspended, but his successor is ineffective. Cronauer continues to pursue Trinh and is eventually persuaded to return to work after a convoy of soldiers encourages him to perform an impromptu broadcast for them before they go off to war. Cronauer is sent out into the field and forced to hide in the bush from the Vietcong; Tuan finds him again and rescues him. He is then revealed as a VC member, which means Cronauer must depart with an honourable discharge if he goes quietly; the vengeful Dickerson is then transferred away as well. Cronauer departs, and Garlick (Forest Whitaker) takes his position.

The movie was a huge success. Robin received a Golden Globe nomination for his portrayal and was nominated for an Oscar (which he did not receive, but he did not have to wait long), a Bafta, and a Sant Jordi Award in Barcelona for Best Foreign Actor. The film and various members of the team went on to win further prizes. Furthermore, the reviews praised it: "Make no mistake: Mr. Williams' performance, while full of raucous comedy, is the product of a skilled actor. In The New York Times, Vincent Canby commented, "Good Morning, Vietnam is one man's tour de force." It was dubbed "the best military comedy since M*A*S*H" by TIME Magazine. 'From the beginning, the film knocks you over with excitement, and for those who can latch on, it's a nonstop trip,' Variety said. 'The ultimate showcase for Robin Williams and his unparalleled ability as a comedy performer,' remarked Flux Capacitor's Stephen Carty.

Other evaluations were even more detailed. 'Levinson's Vietnam seriocomedy is first and mainly a star vehicle for comic Robin Williams, who offers a frenetic, highly charged performance as the real-life DJ Adrian Cronauer in the early years of the War,' stated Emanuel Levy, an American cinema critic and academic. 'The film is a stuffy drama with only cliched insights into the conflict. But Williams' insane speeches behind the microphone are priceless,' said Geoff Andrew in Time Out. 'Good Morning, Vietnam demonstrated to James Plath in Movie Metropolis that Robin Williams could act and be hilariously amusing in the same film,' he wrote. And so it continued.

Despite his desire to be considered seriously as an actor, Williams said that the film's popularity was due to the fact that he was essentially portraying himself. 'Until this role, acting and comedy in cinema were pretty much distinct,' he told The New York Times in 1988. 'As filmmaker Barry Levinson would say, "You don't have to be funny here." I used to think to myself, "I'll push it, I'll make it funnier."

And he was positive that the therapy had contributed to his success. 'It allowed me to display more vulnerability, which I believe the camera captured. 'I think treatment helped me bring out a deeper level of comedy,' he admitted. '[Success] propels you further up the food chain. It's similar to life in the Precambrian sea. There is a screenplay food chain, and success can provide you access to better scripts.'

It was all the better, he remarked, because 'it's a difficult film to categorise. I mean, how do you describe the humorous and serious aspects? It's a comedy-drama. But no! It's a comedy about midgets! No! No, it's a tragic farce! No, it's not a black comedy! So, what exactly is it?'

He was thrilled that Vietnam veterans like it as well. 'No one has ever said, "Hey, I was there in '65 and you weren't, and you can't do that movie." Because we are a country geared toward triumph, toward winning, and we were not victorious, there is still a lot of ambivalence regarding the war... My draft number was 351, and they only took 120 people. I was a very fortunate little white boy! With my draft number, you'd be fighting the V.C. when they came east on Mulholland Drive.'

'I would have probably joined,' he remarked. 'My father was a Navy officer, and my brother was an Air Force officer.'

Finally, he achieved the success he desired. Good Morning, Vietnam is still regarded as one of his career highlights.

Robin and Valerie divorced in 1988. The exact terms of the settlement are unknown, although it is believed that she received $50,000 per month for life (Williams was becoming an extremely wealthy man) and a one-time payment of more than $518,000 from a profit-sharing plan he had set up. But, again, the circumstances were highly tangled. 'Sure, I'm pleased with the film,' he told People. 'But right now, my personal life is like a haemophiliac in a razor factory.' He wasn't kidding when he said that this had been developing for a while.

Marsha Garces was partly Filipino when she was born on June 18, 1956. Leon Garces, her father, was born in Ubay, Bohol, and came to the United States in 1929, subsequently serving in the US Navy during WWII. Ina Rachel Mattila, her mother, was Finnish. Marsha grew up in Shorewood, Wisconsin, and studied painting before working as a waitress and having two brief marriages. Then, in 1984, she went to work as a nanny for the Williams family's baby Zak.

Robin was going through some difficulties at the time, as his marriage was becoming increasingly strained, but it is widely assumed that the romance began around 1986, when Marsha officially became his secretary. Robin and Valerie discreetly divorced in 1987, with Zak receiving split custody, and it was likely inevitable that he and Marsha would marry. She was 'the one who makes my heart sing,' he stated.

Whatever the merits and wrongs of it were, Robin was clearly overjoyed. 'Marsha is Robin's anchor,' claimed his former co-star and friend Pam Dawber. 'She represents realism. Zero hour. She's quite rational, which is exactly what he requires. She's also quite loving. And guarding. She understands who is bad for him and who is good for him, and she works to keep the good relationships going.'

And she was in Thailand with him for the filming of Good Morning, Vietnam. 'She was the hardest-working individual on the set,' said producer Mark Johnson. She was available to him around the clock. 'She adores him.' Marsha was also there for him when Robin's father died in 1987. The couple may have had a strained relationship, but the loss of a parent is always terrible, and Robin needed all the help she could get.

Because there was a youngster in the photo, everyone tried to be as civilised as possible. 'He's absolutely fantastic,' Robin said to People magazine in 1988, describing him as "the most sobering and wonderful thing in my life." Blond. Valerie's eyes are blue. It's my chin. Lips are plump. He resembles an Aryan poster child. He has a vivid imagination and a penchant for numbers. He sometimes reminds me of a forty-year-old Jewish accountant. He can be like Damien from The Omen at times. He has the appearance of an angel without wings at times. He is always aware of how he is feeling. I took him to a diner for lunch today. It was noisy, and he dislikes noise. "We should come back when it's not so crowded," he added diplomatically. He's also not Mr. Outdoors. When I took him camping, he told me, "We've got to find a room with a full refrigerator."

But how was Zak handling everything now? 'He's incredibly adaptable,' Robin insisted, 'and we're all working hard to make the arrangement work. Zachary adores us all, and we adore him. Also, we're all in therapy, which has greatly aided us - Jesus, I should get a discount! Valerie and I are also on the same wavelength. The breakup was painful, but also compassionate. That is preferable to going at each other's throats.'

Valerie agreed. 'Robin has been behaving extremely well,' she told People. 'We're working together in Zach's best interests. We split apart to reflect on our lives. It's a moment for both of us to grow personally. 'I see another man,' says David Sheff, a journalist, 'but I live alone, and I enjoy it that way.'

So the divorce was finalised, but no matter how civilised everyone involved was, there was criticism from some corners. Over time, Robin endeavoured to debunk a particular myth once and for all. 'Marsha did not end my first marriage,' he explained to another journalist. 'It was shattered before we fell in love, and Valerie had already found someone else. Marsha is the person who helped me put my life back together. 'She's a sweet, wonderful soul,' he told the Los Angeles Times.

Following the success of Good Morning, Vietnam, Williams took part in what can only be described as a horrible decision in retrospect. But it's also easy to see why it seemed so brilliant on paper at first. In November 1988, he and another outstanding actor and comic Steve Martin appeared in Samuel Beckett's classic drama Waiting For Godot at New York's Lincoln Center. Mike Nichols directed the seven-week engagement, which sold out so quickly that tickets were never made available to the general public. It was a financial success, at the very least.

The logic was obvious: two brilliant comics who were also players in a darkly funny play about the futility of human existence; two tramps waiting for Godot, who never arrived. And there were plenty of precedents for this: it was not uncommon for major Hollywood stars to appear in low-key stage shows, if for no other reason than to demonstrate their ability. They also tended to take incredibly low pay, primarily to demonstrate that they were willing to suffer for their work (and that they didn't need the money!). But if there is one playwright you should never try to improvise with, it is Samuel Beckett, whose every comma is meticulously planned in advance. And this is where Williams erred.

The critics were harsh. 'But their unsatisfied need to be recognized and their feeling of existence as continual diminishment should seem universal,' observed TIME Magazine's William A. Henry III. 'Instead, the twentieth century's supreme existentialist tragedy has been reduced to a pleasant cabaret routine about the homeless. Williams is the main offender. Williams enacts the audience's supposed frustration at having to ponder when the slave Lucky delivers a long, impassioned speech, a stream of debased knowledge. He dashes away. He stomps on the ground. He shoves a large bone into the slave's hands as if it were an Oscar, telling him to "thank the Academy." Williams leans over Martin, repeating the pet name "Didi, Didi," before launching into The Twilight Zone theme. Martin is never as ridiculous as his character, but his usual cool-guy stride and laid-back vocalisms preclude him from fully entering the role.' Ouch!

'The play has new lines inserted into it, all vulgarisms and completely unnecessary,' fumed John Simon in NewYork Magazine. 'Many are stated throughout Lucky's monologue by Vladimir and Estragon to discourage the speaker. Coyote jawbones become a cinematic clapper in Estragon's hands, or Yorick's skull, as Robin Williams mutters a Hamletic "Alas!" He also carries a gigantic bone with Oscar-appropriate wording and goes through his normal vocal acts, doing a buzzer on a TV game show, a spoof on Twilight Zone menacing music, and all sorts of trick voices, as if this were Good Morning, Godot.' Oh my goodness!

'Turning Beckett's feast of agnostic sarcasm into a series of revue sketches threatened to reduce Godot to nothing more than a vehicle for Martin's and Williams' favourite routines,' W. J. Weatherby observed in the Guardian. 'Steve Martin recently transformed Cyrano de Bergerac into a contemporary American with a large nose in a film, and he has now done the same with Vladimir. Because Mike Nichols did not storm the stage and demand to know what the hell Williams was doing, his improvisations were apparently OK by the director. But one worries if the author will have a negative reaction when the news reaches him in Paris.'

The Financial Times' Frank Lipsius was a little gentler. 'But does the nonchalance of their trendy and cynical generation do Beckett justice?' he said. 'The answer is yes, despite liberties that the author would not surely frown upon, as he is a legendary perfectionist when it comes to productions of his plays. There is only one false note, which occurs at the close of Act One, when Robin Williams as Estragon groans excessively as the lights dim on their inability to move. Throughout the show, however, Williams performs a complete pantomime with just passing references to the text. When Vladimir rushes out the door, Williams follows him, laughingly lifting his leg and scratching the ground like a dog. He picks up a steer skull and addresses it in the manner of Hamlet, or moves the jaws in the manner of a ventriloquist. To persuade Lucky to stop talking, he yells, "You're a liberal!" in mockery of the presidential campaign.

Williams, fresh off the success of Good Morning, Vietnam, and Martin were unused to such a reaction. It evidently hurt, and Robin returned to the matter years later. 'Painful,' he admitted to Playboy. 'We stuck our asses out and got kicked as a result. Some evenings, I'd improvise a little, which irritated die-hard Beckett fans. It wasn't existential; we played it as a comedy team. Like these two vaudeville performers who would break into angst-filled acts. Essentially, it's Laurel and Hardy, as Beckett staged it in Germany.'

But he didn't have to be concerned. After a rough few years of drying out, divorce, lawsuits, remarriage, and finally, the smash movie he'd been waiting for, Robin Williams was still one of the world's hottest names. Everyone wanted a piece of him and was clamouring to sign him up, so he had his pick of the scripts in front of him now. He would go on to make a slew of bad movies, veering way too far into the emotional, but for the time being, he was on a roll. And his best performance was yet to come.

Chapter 8.

IN HIS PRIME

Aside from the disaster that was Waiting for Godot, Robin Williams was at the pinnacle of his career in the late 1980s and early 1990s, delivering some of his best work. It was as if Good Morning, Vietnam had unlocked the floodgates: after years of believing he would never fulfil his full potential, now the successes were pouring in thick and fast. He was to make almost sixty pictures in total, some of which were unforgettable or, in some people's opinion, way too sentimental, but the most notable rate right up there with the best films ever made. And Dead Poets Society (1989) is without a doubt one among them.

The film, directed by Peter Weir and written by Tom Schulman, is set in the Welton Academy in 1959 and tells the story of an inspirational teacher, John Keating (Williams), who challenges traditional teaching practices. Neil Perry (Robert Sean Leonard), Todd Anderson (Ethan Hawke), Knox Overstreet (Josh Charles), Charlie Dalton (Gale Hansen), Richard Cameron (Dylan Kussman), Steven Meeks (Allelon Ruggiero), and Gerard Pitts (James Waterston) are some of his classmates. Captain, please!'It's an allusion to a Walt Whitman poem,' he says. He then convinces them to rip out the first few pages of their poetry textbook!

When the guys discover that Keating is a previous alumni, they reconstitute a society that Keating formerly belonged to, the Dead Poets Society, which meets in secret. Meanwhile, Keating encourages everyone to discover their inner potential while assisting Anderson with a writing task. Dalton publishes an article in which he suggests that girls be allowed to the school and is penalised as a result. Overstreet falls in love and uses poetry to court his lover. Perry aspires to be an actor and participates in a play of A Midsummer Night's Dream against the stated wishes of his father, who confronts Keating before pulling his son from school and promising him a job in medicine at Harvard. Perry eventually kills himself. Cameron blames Keating and reveals the existence of the Dead Poets Society during the course of the investigation. Dalton hits him and is ejected. Headmaster Nolan (Norman Lloyd) summons Anderson to his office, forces him to admit to being a member of the society, and then forces him to sign a statement accusing Keating of inciting Perry to disregard his father's wishes. Keating is then let go.

Keating visits the class to collect a few items after Nolan takes over the English class and realises that the introduction to the poetry book is missing. Anderson informs him that he was compelled to sign the document and, as Nolan orders him to be silent, climbs on his desk and yells, "O Captain!" Captain, please!', Nolan informs him that he will be ejected if he does not sit down. The other boys ignore him and clamber onto their desks, their gaze fixed on Keating. He moves, having changed the boys' lives and making them aware of their own potential.

It was one of Williams' finest achievements, a heartwarming story (even if it managed to indicate that originality and inspirational teaching will get you fired if you're the instructor and cause death if you're the student). The reviewer for the Washington Post termed it "solid, smart entertainment" and praised Robin for her "nicely restrained acting performance." The New York Times' Vincent Canby praised his "exceptionally fine performance," noting that "Dead Poets Society is far less about Keating than about a handful of impressionable boys." 'Robin Williams' performance is more graceful than anything he's done before - he's totally, concentratedly there - [he] reads his lines stunningly, and when he mimics various actors reciting Shakespeare there's no undue clowning in it; he's a gifted teacher demonstrating his skills,' said Pauline Kael.

Roger Ebert was more sceptical, fearing that Williams' humorous persona might seep into the acting and referring to the film as a "collection of pious platitudes... The movie pays lip service to qualities and values that, on the evidence of the screenplay itself, it is cheerfully willing to abandon."

The awards began to pour in. Dead Poets Society won the Academy Award for Best Original Screenplay, and Williams, director Peter Weir, and the picture itself all received nominations. Various Bafta prizes and nominations followed, as did international recognition. 'Carpe diem,' as the saying goes. Take advantage of the opportunity, lads. Make your life extraordinary,' was named the American Film Institute's 95th greatest movie quote. Even the title was justified; there had been concerns that it would be difficult to market to the general public, with actor and producer Harrison Ford commenting that the only worse title he could think of was Dead Poets Society in Winter - yet it had succeeded.

Peter Weir admitted that he had to keep Williams on a leash. In 1989, he told Premiere magazine, "Keating's humour had to be part of his personality." 'Robin and I agreed from the beginning that he would not be an entertainment in the classroom. That would have been inappropriate for the overall tone of the film. It would have been so simple for him to have the youngsters doubling over with laughter. So he had to put the brakes on at times.' However, in the Shakespeare moment, he let the actor loose: 'I had two cameras going, obviously, and I just said, "Boys, this is not a written scene. Treat Robin as your teacher and react accordingly, and remember that it's 1959."' Weir's other innovation was to gather the seven young actors who played the students together and get them to play sports before filming began in order to create a bond between them that was essential for the film.

Meanwhile, Robin, the hour's undisputed hero, was walking on air. His personal life was also improving: on 30 April 1989, he married Marsha, and she soon gave birth to his daughter, Zelda Rae Williams. Zelda was famously named after Princess Zelda of 'The

Legend of Zelda' video-game series - Robin was an avid gamer till the end of his life, so much so that some people suspected it contributed to his sadness - but he later stated that it was Zak's idea. He was, nonetheless, overjoyed. Cody Alan Williams, the couple's second child, was born in 1991.

Robin was now working on a number of high-profile films. Awakenings (1990) followed, based on the true story of British neurologist Oliver Sacks, who in the film is transformed into an American named Malcolm Sayer (Williams), who discovers that the drug L-dopa (also known as levodopa) can be used to treat those who survived the 1917-28 Encephalitis Lethargica (EL) epidemic. Patients, including Robert De Niro's character Leonard Lowe, were awoken after decades of catatonia. Penny Marshall, an old acquaintance of John Belushi, directed it.

While it was a challenging subject, the overall view was that it was handled with care. Sayer discovers that certain patients can respond to particular types of stimuli, such as when a ball is tossed at them or when they hear familiar music. An Ouija board is used to contact Leonard. As the patients gradually regain consciousness, Leonard develops romantic feelings for the daughter of another patient, while also beginning to rebel against the hospital's constraints and causing some disruption in the process. But then his body begins to deteriorate once more, and everyone realises that the drug's impact is only temporary. The term 'awakenings' is understood to have a different connotation in the film when Sayer, a chronically timid guy, asks a nurse out for coffee and the medical staff begins to treat the patients, who were previously catatonic, with increased respect.

There was yet another deluge of positive feedback. 'I read it after seeing Awakenings to learn more about what happened in that Bronx hospital,' Roger Ebert wrote in the Chicago Sun-Times. 'What both the film and the book express is the enormous courage of the patients and the profound experience of their doctors, as they're-experienced in a little manner what it is to be born, to open your eyes and learn to your shock that "you " are alive.'

In New York Magazine, David Denby stated, "Awakenings was made with sensitivity and taste." 'There is no blatant exploitation, and nothing in the sensational, brazen style of One Flew Over the Cuckoo's Nest (the ideological nuthatch bash's high reputation astounds me). The patients are always portrayed as persons, not as spectacles, despite the fact that the strangeness and tension of their clinical symptoms are the most arresting aspects of the film... As conceived by playwright Steven Zaillian, Sayer needs waking. He is a man with a fundamental aspect missing: he is shy and guarded, kind but shut off, and asexual. Williams does some serious work after dropping the charming Pied Piper shtick that made his performances in Good Morning, Vietnam and Dead Poets Society so boring. He hunches slightly and clutches his arms at his sides, as if he's attempting to keep cold air from sliding up his abdomen.'

Other detractors were persuaded, albeit with doubts. 'There's a visceral, subversive element to De Niro's performance: he doesn't hesitate from making Leonard seem hideous,' noted Entertainment Weekly's Owen Gleiberman. 'Yet, unlike the much superior Rain Man, Awakenings isn't actually structured around the eccentricity of its primary character. Leonard is viewed solemnly in the film, and he is transformed into an icon of emotion. Even if you're captivated by the acting (as I was), you may find yourself resisting the film's design.'

'I suppose in an uncanny manner, De Niro did somehow feel his way into becoming Parkinsonian,' says Oliver Sacks, author of the 1973 memoir on which the film is based. So much so that sometimes, after dinner, I'd notice his foot curling or him leaning to one side, as if he couldn't seem to get out of it. I thought the way things were incorporated was strange. At other levels, I believe things were sentimentalised and oversimplified.'

He did, however, enjoy Williams' performance. 'Robin has practically instant access to portions of the mind that most of us don't have - dreamy parts with phantasmagoric associations,' he told New York Magazine. 'Robin becoming other people reminds me of Theodore Hook, the early-nineteenth-century wit who could improvise operas, playing every part. He was the most popular man in London, and he was regularly invited to dinner and performances. The need for Hook, like Robin, never stopped. Hook, on the other hand, never had the opportunity for calm inwardness since he drank frequently and died in his forties. Robin's brilliance, on the other hand, is much more under control. He's not in its clutches.' It was a foreshadowing of what was to come two and a half decades later.

But the admiration was mutual, with Robin citing this role as his favourite of all time in a 2013 Reddit interview. 'I think playing Oliver Sacks in Awakenings was a gift because it gave me the opportunity to meet him and explore the human brain from the inside out,' he said. 'Because Oliver writes subjectively about human behaviour, and that was the beginning of my fascination with human behaviour.'

Meanwhile, critics continued to weigh in, with Desson Howe of the Washington Post saying, 'when [Sayers' love interest] nurse Julie Kavner (another former TV being) delivers the main Message (life, she tells Williams, is "given and taken away from all of us"), it doesn't sound like the climactic point of a great movie. It sounds more like a line from one of Laverne & Shirley's more sensitive episodes.'

The New York Times' Janet Maslin wrote, 'Awakenings works harder at achieving such misplaced liveliness than at winning its audience over in other ways.'

Williams was widely regarded as an outstanding actor by this point, but his next choice surprised many: playing a grown-up Peter Pan in

Hook (1991). It's possible that he accepted the role because he'd never seen a production of the play before: he saw it for the first time at the age of thirty-eight, after director Steven Spielberg had already cast him. It has a fantastic cast, including Dustin Hoffman as Captain Hook, Julia Roberts as Tinkerbell, Bob Hoskins as Smee, and Maggie Smith as Granny Wendy, but the conceit that Peter has grown up and forgotten his own childhood was too much for some. The villainous Hook kidnaps his family, and Peter must return to Neverland to save them, but the story falls flat. The film was a commercial success (though not as much as predicted) but a critical failure, and in a career full of hits and misses, this one definitely fell into the latter category.

This unexpected flop was almost immediately compensated for when Williams made The Fisher King (1991), which some consider to be his best film. It was a fantasy offering directed by Terry Gilliam and written by Richard LaGravenese that could easily have gone off the rails but did not. It concerned Jack Lucas (Jeff Bridges), a shock jock whose on-air utterances prompt someone to commit mass murder in a Manhattan bar. Lucas becomes a hopeless drunk, working in a record store with his girlfriend Anne, before being attacked by a group of thugs. He is rescued by Parry (Williams), a homeless man looking for the Holy Grail. Initially, Jack is cautious but then discovers that Parry had been rendered catatonic for a time after seeing his wife murdered by the same psycho who carried out the bar killing (and had previously called Lucas). Parry is haunted by a hallucination of a Red Knight, of which he is terrified. He tells Jack the story of the Fisher King, who was charged with guarding the Holy Grail.

Jack wants to redeem himself for inadvertently having caused the killings. He introduces Parry to Lydia (Amanda Plummer), an accountant who Parry has a crush on, and they fall in love. But Parry sees the Red Knight and flees, only to run into the same thugs who had gone after Jack. They beat him and he returns to a catatonic state. To help him, Jack breaks into the house of a famous architect and takes possession of a simple trophy that Parry believes to be the Grail: in so doing, he prevents the suicide of the architect by tripping the alarm. He takes the trophy to Parry, who regains consciousness and is reunited with Lydia. Finally, Jack tells Anne he loves her and they embrace.

This was not one of Williams' major box-office successes, although it performed perfectly respectably, but the critics loved it. 'The Fisher King has two actors at the top of their form, and a compelling, well-directed and well-produced story,' said Variety. 'Visually impressive, frequently pretentious, and extremely fluid as narrative (the 137 minutes sail by effortlessly), this mythic comedy-drama presents Gilliam as half seer, half snake-oil salesman and defies you to sort out which is which,' wrote Jonathan Rosenbaum in the Chicago Reader. 'Although there are moments when the mixture of comedy, fantasy and drama don't come off, this is still an original, touching movie that is well worth the price of a ticket,' opined Jo Berry in Empire Magazine.

'Working within the constraints of a big studio film has brought out Gilliam's best: he's become a true storyteller and a wonderful director of actors. This time he delights not only the eye but the soul,' said David Ansen in Newsweek. 'A touching and funny one-of-a-kind gem about two lost souls who help each other find redemption. Bridges once again proves what an underappreciated actor he is, while Williams is at his manic best,' said Chuck O'Leary of FulvueDrive-In.com. 'The Fisher King emphasises the purpose of fairy tales in our lives, and the way a fantasy can help us see reality more clearly,' said Jeffrey Overstreet.

The film resulted in another Oscar nomination for Williams (who, by now, must have been feeling always the bridesmaid, never the bride), while his co-star Mercedes Ruehl, who played Anne, won the Oscar for Best Supporting Actress, as well as a number of other awards. There was a score of further Oscar nominations for the movie and the usual international suspects, with Williams getting a Golden Globe Award for Best Actor on the back of his performance. Terry Gilliam, meanwhile, won the People's Choice Award from the Toronto International Film Festival for what had been a stunningly original take on what was actually Arthurian legend. It was another triumph all round.

The hits and misses continued. Next up was Toys (1992), another fantasy film with a fine cast, including Michael Gambon, Joan Cusack, Robin Wright and Jamie Foxx in his film debut, all about a childlike man who owns a toy factory. 'Toys is a very whimsical, strange feast, almost a nonmusical musical,' Williams told The New York Times. 'I hope people enjoy the ride.' But they didn't – the film was regarded as a failure, both critically and commercially, with the director Barry Levinson seen as partly to blame. Given that he had also directed Good Morning, Vietnam (and Rain Man in 1988), it was unclear why the project had gone so badly wrong.

'[What made the film] that much sadder a failure is that everyone involved must have sincerely felt they were doing the Lord's work, care and concern going hand in hand with an almost total miscalculation of mood,' said Kenneth Turan in the Los Angeles Times. 'Even Robin Williams, so lively a voice in Aladdin, is on beatific automatic pilot here, preferring to be warm and cuddly when a little of his energy (paradoxically on splendid display in the film's teaser trailer) is desperately called for. The Grinch Who Stole Christmas seems to have stripped the life from this film as well, leaving a pretty shell, expensive but hollow, in its place.'

'To cut Toys a minor break, it is ambitious,' wrote Peter Travers in Rolling Stone. 'It is also a gimmicky, obvious and pious bore, not to mention overproduced and overlong.'

But for every miss there was a hit. Williams had, indeed, starred in the aforementioned Aladdin (1992), or at least voiced his part: the role of Genie/Merchant had been written specifically with him in mind – a risk, as he took a lot of persuading before he would accept. He didn't want to work for Disney, he said, with the result that two of the writers, Ron Clements and John Musker, who were also the producers and directors, created a reel of animation of the Genie, which they allied to Robin's real life stand-up. When they showed it to him, he thought it was so funny that he agreed to do the film. He also improvised a great deal of his part, contributing up to thirty hours on tape that had to be cut down to fit the movie, impersonating numerous others in the process, including Jack Nicholson, Carol Channing, Ethel Merman, William F. Buckley Jr., Robert De Niro ('Are you talkin' to me?') and Pinocchio. 'I was improvising, and the animators came in and laughed, and it just grew,' he told New York Magazine. 'In times like this, when there's so much crap running around, it's great to laugh and be free. I felt wonderful; that's why I did it. And it was such a pleasure when it came out and people said, "I loved it as much as my kid did." But then some things happened later on.' A veritable tour de force, it was estimated that, in total, Williams improvised about fifty-two different voices. In the event, Aladdin was the most successful film of 1992. Unusually for Robin, who was on the whole considered to be an easy person to work with, the movie generated some bad feeling on the part of all those involved because of the events that happened later on. For various reasons, related to the fact that Toys was coming out around the same time, Williams demanded that his name and image would not be used for marketing and would not take more than 25 percent of marketing space. The studio did not stick to the letter of the deal, using his voice to sell merchandise of the products, leading to a very public and bitter row between the two of them, with Robin, who had taken a much smaller fee than usual (this was normal for a voiceover), refusing to do any promotion. What this essentially boiled down to was that he said he'd do the film if they didn't present it as a Robin Williams' vehicle, which they then did.

It ended in Disney publicly apologising to Robin (and giving him a Picasso then valued at $1 million and no doubt worth considerably more now) but it was an unhappy episode that left an unpleasant taste in the mouth. 'It wasn't as if we hadn't set it out,' he said. 'I don't want to sell stuff. It's the one thing I don't do. In Mork & Mindy, they did Mork dolls – I didn't mind the dolls; the image is theirs. But the voice, that's me; I gave them myself. When it happened, I said, "You know I don't do that." And they apologised; they said it was done by other people.'

In his spare time, Robin was still doing stand-up, an act that he pretty much imported onto his numerous chat-show appearances, which were fast becoming known as being quite as enjoyable as watching his act. In 1992 he appeared on The Arsenio Hall Show and spoke of it in much the same way as he did his actual act: 'Going on stage is part catharsis for me, but it's almost trying to work out my own fears,' he told The New York Times shortly after he returned from a trip to the UK.

The interview was also an explanation as to quite how much current affairs informed his act. 'Tonight I was jet-lagged, but I just wanted to explode with all this information,' he said of his appearance on the show. 'You want to talk about the marines in Somalia hitting the beach and meeting the press. "All right, Colonel, I want you to take out that camera position. Get away, son! He's got a flashbulb!" And, like, the royal family. I was in England and Windsor Castle was burning down and, like, it's not insured. Oh, damn, I'm sorry! Let the people pay 8 billion crowns. And there's no sprinkler system. Oh rot!'

Entertaining stuff but there was also a truly manic quality to it – this was a newspaper interview, after all. But it seemed as if Robin just couldn't turn off the tap: something inside was relentless, pushing him to be funny even when he didn't have to be. It was the mark of a comic genius, all right – but it wasn't healthy and didn't give the impression of a man at peace with himself.

Then again, there were certainly some things he could be pretty serious about and, at that stage, Marsha was one of them. The relationship was very strong then, with Robin crediting her with pulling him through a very difficult time and he fiercely resented the picture that had been painted of him running off with the nanny. Indeed, he blamed it on a piece in People Magazine.

'It was an ambush by them,' he told The New York Times in 1992. 'It's very destructive. It still is. There are still nanny jokes. You want to go out and yell.

'There was an article about men who leave their wives when they become famous. And I wanted to write to this man and say, "Listen, you may have your ridiculous theories, but the truth is my wife left me." My marriage had been in shambles for some time. Marsha just basically started to talk to me and said: "Listen jerk, what are you having these ridiculous affairs for? What are you yelling and screaming about? Wake up!" Slowly I began realising I'm a decent person, and everything wonderful that has happened to my life is because of her. It's hideous that she takes the rap as a homewrecker, which is a lie. It's the exact opposite. She has taken me from zero to the sky.' It was an unusually impassioned outburst and, for Robin to complain about anyone making jokes, when he so often mercilessly harpooned the pompous himself, showed that this had left some real scars. For him, it was yet another sign that fame had its downside: people took an interest in your private life and made remarks. Still, he was now top of the Hollywood A-list, enjoying the fruits of his success and a seriously rich man. He was about to enjoy some further career highlights in the forthcoming years – but also experienced a terrible tragedy that struck one of his closest friends.

Chapter 9.

TRIUMPH AND TRAGEDY

Williams' cinematic career soared over much of the 1990s. Mrs. Doubtfire, based on Anne Fine's novel Alias Madame Doubtfire and co-starring Sally Field, was another significant part in 1993. Surprisingly, the picture garnered mixed reviews at its initial release, but it is today regarded as one of the great classics, ranking 67th on the American picture Institute's 100 Years, 100 Laughs: America's Funniest Movies and 40th on Bravo's 100 Funniest Movies of All Time. The story of Daniel and Miranda Hillard, divorced parents of three, was told in the film, which also starred Pierce Brosnan in his pre-Bond days. Daniel, by chance, is a voice actor (which provided Robin with numerous opportunities to goof about), so once the divorce is finalised and he has severely limited custody, he disguises himself as a Scottish nanny and worms his way back into his children's lives. All is revealed at the end, and he is forgiven with the message (by this point, many of Williams' films had messages) that not only had he learnt to be a better father, but that family won over all else.

(In a touching example of this being true, a completely unknown actor named Dr. Toad had a bit part as a bartender in the film; in reality, Dr. Toad was none other than R. Todd Williams, now an acclaimed wine maker and co-founder of Toad Hollow Vineyards and Robin's oldest half-brother; he had, indeed, been a bartender in his time.)

And Williams certainly succeeded: his performance was vital to the film's success. 'In the picture, if Robin's character doesn't trick the woman he'd been married to for fourteen years, she won't hire him - and there'd be no movie,' said director Chris Columbus in 1993. But it was considerably more personal than many people realised: Robin had recently gone through a divorce and was well aware of the issues that arise when parents and children do not spend enough time together. In some ways, it was as raw as the stand-up material he'd done about drug use.

Mrs. Doubtfire was frequently likened to Tootsie (1982), a Dustin Hoffman vehicle in which he, too, was dragged up in order to acquire work in a soap opera, but, while Tootsie was rightfully and quickly recognized as a comedy classic, Mrs. Doubtfire was not. It was compared unfavourably to another cross-dressing classic, Some Like It Hot (1959), and even the (sort of) sympathetic reviews were harsh.

'I've rarely laughed so hard at a film I generally loathed,' David Ansen wrote in Newsweek. 'The frock, the mask, and Mrs. Doubtfire's gentility are intrinsically restrictive, but nothing holds Mr. Williams back when he's on a roll,' The New York Times' Janet Maslin wrote. 'Although too sentimental in sections and maybe twenty minutes too long, this Robin Williams-in-drag production offers the comic with a sleek surface for delivering his shtick, within a story with broad family appeal,' wrote Variety's Brian Lowry.

'Sitcom material, then, with laboured comic interludes and a mushy post-feminist mindset. Despite the fact that it's funny,' said Derek Adams in Time Out. 'Williams must break free from his second-rate Tootsie impersonation, ankles clasped in pathos and face coated in latex. 'In the end, he pulls it off, but it's not pretty,' wrote Desson Thomson in the Washington Post. 'You will laugh till your ribs ache - not because director Chris Columbus of the Home Alone movies has a knack for farce, which he does, but because Williams is to comedy what the Energizer Bunny is to batteries,' says the Washington Post. 'He just keeps going and going and going,' Rita Kempley recalled.

But those who actually knew about these things, namely the film industry, recognized its quality right away. For his portrayal, Williams received the Global Globe Award for Best Actor, and the film received the award for Best Film. It was also nominated for an Oscar, although for Best Make-up. Robin was taking it very seriously.

'Here's a guy who lives in a really random way and discovers there's more than him through a difficult journey,' he told New York Magazine. 'And my wife does the same thing. We had an early meeting with the studio; they wanted the pair to reconcile. That is the one myth that most psychiatrists will tell you is repeated by divorced children in therapy - and it is the one that experts do not want to perpetuate. "Have you ever had a memory of your mom and dad together?" they'll ask kids." The kids say no, but it's the larger concept: "They're together." Norman Rockwell sold it to you. "The family, at the table... despite the fact that they're all armed." This film is about true family values. How many fathers simply quit up after a divorce? The natural impulse is to declare, "I love my son," and then withdraw. If you're fortunate, the father will become an uncle. But the strange thing is, he needs his children just as much as they need him.'

Mrs. Doubtfire was to become one of his major triumphs, so much so that there was speculation of a sequel (Robin actually detested sequels) until his death. Several plot concepts were floated, including dressing up as a woman to track down his daughter after she went to college, but nothing seemed quite right. Later, when Williams' career was perhaps not quite as skyrocketing as it had once been, there was even conjecture that another Mrs. Doubtfire could save it. But that was not to be.

Even as late as May 2013, however, the director Chris Columbus was still talking about the idea. '[Robin Williams and I are] talking about a sequel to Mrs. Doubtfire,' he revealed in an interview with the Huffington Post. 'We've talked about it, and the studio is interested in it. The thing that fascinates me about a sequel to Mrs. Doubtfire is with most actors who create an iconic role like Mrs.

Doubtfire, when you come back and recreate that character, well, you're twenty years older so you're not going to look the same. The interesting thing with Mrs. Doubtfire is there's a character, there's a woman, who is genuinely going to appear precisely as she did in 1993. So I look forward to seeing that trailer. That's a great idea, plus there's no CGI. So we just need to make sure that the tale is emotionally compelling, that there's a reason for telling it, and that it's not like Big Momma's House or anything. It must be both passionate and humorous.'

Back in 1993, Robin was figuring out how to deal with his newfound celebrity. That summer, he took his family to an Italian villa and fully disconnected himself from the firm. They were also set to relocate to a sprawling 12,000-square-foot mansion overlooking San Francisco Bay. Marsha was, by now, playing a vital role in Williams' career: understanding his fragility, she worked as a type of 'gatekeeper' to him, shielding him from as much of the industry's pressures as she could.

And she did a lot more than that: before Good Morning, Vietnam, she encouraged Robin to learn about the era's history. She was there on the set of the majority of his films, offering backup and assistance. She sounded like his agent at times: 'Money's never been the motive for me to promote anything,' she told New York Magazine. 'Unless the entire country collapses, we have all we'll ever need,' says one. I'm more interested in what Robin hasn't done and what comes next. I'm biassed, but I've never seen somebody with his range before.'

While others remarked that she was turning into a bossy Hollywood wife, it was actually perfect for Robin. Marsha discovered Mrs. Doubtfire when the two of them established the Blue Wolf production firm to evaluate scripts and identify acceptable projects for him. She was the film's producer, which raised more suspicions, but considering that everything she did was meant to improve her husband's prestige and happiness, the doubters were correct for the second time. She would go on to make more films for him.

But, while things were going well at home, one of Robin's closest friends was about to go through a tremendous tragedy. Christopher Reeve, his old Juilliard buddy, was now just as renowned, but in a different way, having established his reputation in the Superman movie. Riding was one of his passions as an incredibly athletic and enthusiastic man, but in June 1995, he was thrown from his horse and landed on his head. He broke his neck and was paralyzed from the neck down from that point till the end of his life, nine years later.

Of course, it was a sad occurrence for everyone concerned, especially Reeve and his wife Dana. He later admitted to feeling suicidal (and who could blame him?) but vowed to carry on as best he could with the assistance of his wife. In subsequent years, he had no recollection of the event and was first delirious; he was then subjected to an operation to reattach his skull to his spine, which had a 50% chance of success. Even Reeve, who is undeniably brave, would have been taken aback when, in the days leading up to the operation, squat chap' burst in wearing scrubs and spectacles and speaking in a Russian accent. He was going to perform a rectal examination on Reeve, he said. It was, of course, Williams, reprising a tiny role from Hugh Grant's 1995 film Nine Months, and Christopher burst out laughing for the first time since the accident. 'My old friend had helped me know that somehow I was going to be alright,' he said later in his memoirs Still Me.

Christopher Reeve and I both went to Julliard. When I found out about his accident, I was as shocked as everyone else,' Robin subsequently told the Calgary Sun. 'Everyone was so serious. I knew that wasn't good for Chris, so I disguised up as his proctologist and claimed to be him. The look on his face nearly destroyed my heart. He has told me ever since that he wanted to live because he was able to laugh again.'

But Robin did so much more than make Christopher chuckle. It was never revealed to what extent this occurred, but it was commonly assumed that he contributed to the cost of Reeve's medical care. He undoubtedly became interested in the Christopher and Dana Reeve Foundation. Dana characterised the two of them as "closer than brothers," and over the years, Robin was frequently seen by his old friend's side. Reeve's dramatic physical metamorphosis revealed much about the life he had abandoned.

In truth, Robin did a lot of charity work behind the scenes. Among the organisations he supported were Comic Relief (for the homeless and Hurricane Katrina victims), Médecins Sans Frontières, Operation Smile, the Pediatric AIDS Association, Challenged Athletes Foundation, St. Jude Children's Research Hospital, the Make-a-Wish Foundation (some of the children featured in Patch Adams, 1998), Project Open Hand, Glide, The Gorilla Foundation, Seacology, River of Words, God's Love We Deliver, Women at Ground Zero,

He was also a frequent visitor to San Francisco hospitals' children's wards. 'I generally go around Christmas,' he explained to the Calgary Sun. 'I ride a bike attached to an IV. I used to be a big hit when I did Mork, but now they like it when I do Mrs. Doubtfire.'

His motivation was radically different from that of many celebrities who conduct good activities primarily to boost their own public image. Williams had come from a wealthy family to begin with, and now he was extremely affluent (it was believed that he earned $29 million in just two years in the early 1990s, which was worth much more then than it is today). And he went above and beyond what many others do. He made benefit appearances to support literacy and women's rights, and he worked extensively with the United Service Organizations (USO), which provided entertainment for American troops stationed abroad. He was scheduled to entertain 100,000 troops in 13 nations for the USO, including Iraq and Afghanistan. (In this, he was similar to another great American comedic performer,

Bob Hope, who was also a regular with the US Army.)

He and Marsha formed the Windfall Foundation for several charities, which he continued to do for the rest of his life. In December 1999, he sang in French in a BBC-inspired music video featuring international celebrities performing a cover of The Rolling Stones' 'It's Only Rock 'n Roll (But I Like It)' for the charity Children's Promise. Following the 2010 Canterbury earthquake, Williams donated the whole revenues of his Weapons of Self Destruction Christchurch concert to aid in the rebuilding of the New Zealand city (half of the proceeds went to the Red Cross and half to the mayor's building fund). He also donated to St. Jude Children's Research Hospital. After his death, many of the people and charities he had helped came forward to thank him: even his harshest critics had to admit that he was an unusually generous man.

And the movies just kept coming. Some sank without a trace, while others became part of the cultural landscape, such as Jumanji, a 1995 offering that had twelve-year-old Alan Parrish (Williams) trapped in a strange board game called Jumanji in 1969 and only being released as an adult twenty-six years later when two more children began playing the game. But when he comes out, so do all the monsters and terrors who were lurking inside with him. Given Robin's often strained relationship with his own father, it's interesting that the actor who plays his father in the film and subsequently the mad hunter out to catch him are one and the same man: something no one mentions at any point. Williams would have seen the irony.

The picture received both mixed reviews and a lot of money, which meant that anyone who was offended by the reviewers could at least cry all the way to the bank. And that was excellent old-fashioned entertainment. 'It's a machete. Flamethrower! And a nightlight (oh, that's right, I was ten, so maybe I should give up the flamethrower for a Ronson lighter),' Williams remarked on Reddit when asked what he'd take if he had to step into the board game that was Jumanji.

And some of the critics were willing to embrace the amusement factor. 'Take away the CGI mayhem, and what emerges is a pretty sad narrative of second chances and innocence prematurely lost,' remarked BBC.com's Neil Smith. 'A deliberate yet highly entertaining special effects spectacle,' USA Today declared. 'Like the rest of Johnston's career, Jumanji puts vibrant characters through paces that will quicken any child's pulse,' wrote Groucho Reviews' Peter Canavese.

'A visually impressive and exciting adventure that keeps the suspense, thrills, and comedy running high through the shocking ending and delivers compelling characters with moving lights that have the audience rooting,' Boxoffice Magazine's Christine James wrote. 'Everyone is OK here, with Williams taking on the peculiar character of straight man for much of the journey,' said Chris Hicks in the Deseret News. Audiences enjoyed it as well, with Williams playing a sort of Indiana Jones figure, albeit not an archaeologist searching for lost treasures, but rather a regular Joe.

'The movie itself is likely to send younger children fleeing from the theatre, or hiding in their parents' arms,' said famed film reviewer Roger Ebert. Those who do sit through it will most likely toss and turn with nightmares inspired by its terrifying pictures,' he said in the Chicago Sun-Times. 'Whoever believed this was a family film (the MPAA grades it PG - not even PG-13!) must believe that children are made of tough material. The film is a bleak special-effects spectacle full of horrible visuals that instil terror and despair. Even for older audiences, there are few redeeming qualities, because what little story there is works as a coat hook for the f/x sequences, which appear out of nowhere and then vanish.'

Despite this, Jumanji has gone on to become one of the most well-known children's films of all time, and it remains a popular television show.

Williams was a man on the go. The Birdcage, based on the French mega hit La Cage aux Folles, was released in 1996 and told the story of a gay couple: Armand Goldman (Williams), who owns a nightclub, and his companion Albert (Nathan Lane), a drag queen. (Many people were surprised that the casting was not reversed.) Armand has a son, Val (Dan Futterman), who has recently gotten engaged and wants to introduce the two sets of parents, but his fiancée is from a strict family. Much laughter ensues.

Were they concerned that they were portraying homosexuality in a stereotyped way, with a lot of shrieking and camp? 'The compassion of it will assist,' Robin explained to Premiere magazine. 'We may have made some sacrifices, but we attempted to find a pair who were as loving as any heterosexual couple. It's about love. But brace yourself, because there will be individuals who are irritated.'

It also left him in the strange position of having to tone it down while his co-star got to be joyful. Williams was particularly nice about his co-star, maybe realising that this would be difficult for Lane, and that it was he, not Nathan, who would be expected to get everyone laughing. 'Oh, it was pretty hard,' he admitted in a Reddit interview when asked if he was tempted to laugh. 'That character's voice, Agador Spartacus. It wasn't only me who was struggling. [Director] Mike Nichols would laugh so hard that they would have to cover his head with a blanket. Gene Hackman was another hilarious character. His remark about New England's foliage was one of the funniest, driest bits of comedy I'd ever seen.'

The film received generally positive reviews and accolades from the Gay & Lesbian Alliance Against Defamation for 'moving beyond stereotypes to recognize the character's depth and humanity. The film celebrates differences while also highlighting the absurdity of concealing those distinctions'. Perhaps most crucially, at least in the perspective of Hollywood, it made a lot of money. It demonstrated that Williams, even in a gay role, could play the straight man.

In reality, he had been approached to perform the drag role first. He was also requested to return back the prior year in Julie Newmar's To Wong Foo, Thank You For Everything! (1995), but he turned down both roles for the same reason: he didn't want to be typecast after already dressing as a woman in Mrs. Doubtfire. 'My management pleaded with me to play Albert,' he said. 'He claimed it would give me free rein to be the most ridiculous I'd ever been. But I've been a huge terrible woman in the past. For me, the objective was to play the more subtle Armand and see if I could still get some chuckles. It's bad enough that the creators behind Mrs. Doubtfire want to put me back in drag for a sequel. Every other studio in Hollywood requires me to squirm into a bra and pantyhose.'

The never-to-be-made sequel to Mrs. Doubtfire was definitely in the works, but it was evident even at that stage that the producers were struggling to come up with a suitable story.

In contrast to his exceptional professional production, Williams was experiencing a period of tranquillity in his personal life. Most children expect their parents to use humorous voices when reading them a story, but Robin's children told him to calm down. Interviewers began to notice that he wasn't breaking into hilarious voices in the middle of interviews as much as he used to, which was undoubtedly a good indication. Apart from anything else, he was suddenly a parent three times over, and his children expected him to act like one. He and Marsha were very much a team, managing his job, their philanthropic work, and their personal lives. And, as one of the world's most bankable stars, the offers kept coming in. Life was great.

When he starred in Jack (1996), he welcomed comparisons to a great 1988 picture - Big, in which Tom Hanks plays a twelve-year-old in the body of a mature man - in which he portrayed a ten-year-old in the body of a grown man. The confusion in Big was caused by a mystery fortune-teller machine, whereas in Jack it was caused by a premature ageing ailment, but there were clearly parallels, not least because both had to deal with the unpleasant subject of girls.

Robin was hesitant to take on the project at first. 'When Jack's script came to me, I said a loud no,' he told the Calgary Sun. 'I told Disney that I'd been there and done that. I'm 44 years old and furry. The only thing I'm really cut out for is a musical adaptation of Congo. [However], Disney brought forth the big guns. They hired my buddy Francis Ford Coppola to direct, and he told me that I'd never played a part like this before.'

Francis Ford Coppola is a name to be reckoned with. Robin signed the contract and spent the next few weeks connecting with the kid actors who would play Jack's friends, camping, playing baseball, and telling ghost stories. 'It felt like a Lord of the Flies daycare,' he added.

Coppola told the Toronto Sun in 1996, "I came up with this concept to have Robin in a situation with eight or nine nine-year-olds." 'I used to be a camp counsellor, and we performed a variety of activities. On the summit, we ate peanut butter and jelly sandwiches and napped.'

'We nicknamed it Camp Coppola,' Robin added. "We did kid stuff like ride bikes for days and go to toy stores. I'd digested all of this information by the end, which was strange. It was almost like time travel by association. At that age, it's all about the little things - your "stuff," what they have, and friendships. When the world crashes, it absolutely collapses. That's why people cry one minute and feel terrific the next.'

Coppola lavished admiration on Williams, describing him as "childlike but not childish or even remotely a child." His imagination and excitement are what make Robin appear so childish,' he claimed, and both of them took the project so seriously that they enlisted the services of a ten-year-old boy to help him prepare for the role. 'Robin would go through each scene first,' Coppola explained. 'Then his adviser would do it independently while Robin looked on. There were some things the boy did that would astound Robin, and he would change what he was doing.'

The picture, according to the two men, expressed a melancholy in their own childhoods. 'I lived in that large mansion and I was very much alone,' Robin told the Toronto Sun, a solemn tone emerging amid all the hilarity. 'I still went to school, but I was on a vast farm in the country, far away from everyone. I recall being picked on and having to find different routes home because you don't want your ass kicked. I was picked on because I was little. At one point, I felt fat and chubby. That's why I started wrestling in high school. At the very least, if you're only 103 pounds, you can kick another 103-pound guy's ass.'

Coppola didn't seem to have much fun as a child either. 'I believe Hemingway stated that to be a great artist, you have to have a terrible childhood,' he explained. 'I got polio as a child and was barred from having any interaction with children. There was a lot of longing going on. And I believe that is why I related to this picture.

'I read Jack's script with Robin in mind. And it reminded me of Kafka's Metamorphosis. "It'll be fine if you accept him as a giant cockroach," I said. The idea collapses if you don't accept Robin as a 10-year-old.'"

But the audience accepted Robin as a youngster because they had done so in many of his earlier appearances, whether or not he was playing a child. But by this point, Williams was in his forties, married with children, and a serious A-lister. He had, without a doubt, matured.

Chapter 10.

PICASSOS AND PRINCES

It didn't take long for things to calm down with Disney: to be fair, it made no sense for either party if a major star and a large film business continued to dispute. In any case, they wanted Williams to return to work for them. Robin responded in his usual rambling manner. 'No, I don't have a Disney contract,' he told the Toronto Sun. 'In fact, they have a contract with me. Tony, a male, has been following me around. [Mafioso voice]: "I'd like you to quit talking about Mr. Eisner. "He has the warmth of a snow pea." "You mocked the King!"We'd like to speak with you outside, Robin."

'Merchandising tie-ins, the works. 'I don't mind if they manufacture dolls,' he went on to say. 'It's when they use my voice that it gets fascinating,' said Picasso, albeit Robin's version of events differed slightly. 'The issue is, they didn't give me a Picasso as a punishment for breaking the deal,' he went on. 'The Picasso arrived first, then they broke the arrangement, and finally we divorced. Then they apologised, which was all I needed. "We violated the agreement, and then we put out a press campaign that made it appear as if you were sticking us up for money," I wanted them to say. Studios do this all the time, but they simply don't admit it. "Shhh! Do you mean a lie?"But they did, and they admitted it, and we're back now." It was difficult for a while. "Daddy's fighting with Disney, so we won't be going to Orlando for a while," you explain to the kids. There will be no more plush toys, Hunchback bags, or anything."

Williams, by the way, was paid $75,000 for a picture that grossed over $600 million at the box office, but that wasn't the point: the principle was at risk.

But, just in time for an Aladdin sequel, Aladdin and the King of Thieves (1996), everyone had kissed and made up. This was not the first sequel - that had been The Return of Jafar (1994), with the Blue Genie voiced by Dan Castellaneta (Homer Simpson), when emotions were still running high - and it was being made for the video market rather than the cinema, but it was in everyone's best interests to re-engage Williams. In reality, a third of the animation for the film had already been completed using Castellaneta, but when Robin joined on, everyone was eager to start over.

'It's a much stronger film with Robin,' Ann Daly, president of Buena Vista Home Video, told TV Guide in 1996. 'It takes the project to a higher level. Nobody can match him in the recording studio. He inspired the animators.' (It seemed a little unfair to Castellaneta, but that's showbiz.)

In 1997, Williams gave the performance that landed him an Oscar in Good Will Hunting, the film that also launched the careers of Matt Damon and, to a lesser extent, Ben Affleck (who had already made a name for himself), though the award was for Best Supporting Actor rather than the lead role. The narrative, created by Affleck and Damon, features Damon as Will Hunting, a mathematical prodigy who works as a blue-collar worker. After his abilities are revealed, he is almost imprisoned for assaulting a police officer, but is released if he agrees to study mathematics with a prominent professor (Stellan Skarsgrd) and consults a therapist, Sean Maguire (Williams), who has also dealt with numerous troubles in his past. Will is then able to reassess his life and begin to establish a name for himself.

The picture was a huge success, one of Williams' largest in his career, grossing over $225 million in theatres and collecting nine Oscar nominations. Along with Robin, Affleck and Damon were nominated for Best Original Screenplay. It was one of those films that was adored by both audiences and critics.

'Damon and Affleck were wise enough to realise that writing terrific parts for themselves would not get their script filmed,' said Quentin

Curtis in the Daily Telegraph in 1998. 'They wanted a big star, so they dangled the idea of a terrific supporting role in front of the A-listers. Will's psychiatrist, whose own life has gone off the rails, plays the role and prods Will toward maturity. Robin Williams bit the bait, and he gets to deliver two speeches that appear like they'll be used as audition pieces for actors: one about the virtue of imperfection, and the other a nasty lecture to Will on the difference between knowledge and experience.'

'The strength of Good Will Hunting comes in the incredible assurance of its storyline, as well as the support given to it by both its cast and makers,' observed Empireonline. 'Director Van Sant avoids needless sentiment, preferring to locate the emotional reality and severity within the story. Damon is fantastic, and Affleck is as so. However, in a film that emanates quality, it is Robin Williams who delivers both the heart and the spotlight - the Oscar was totally merited in this case.'

'Mr. 'Williams is marvellously solid and robust here; Mr. Damon, very much the supernova, is erratic in ways that make his role continuously unexpected,' observed The New York Times' Janet Maslin. 'The screenplay's strongest moments occur in a couple of big, defining speeches (particularly one from Sean in the Boston Public Gardens) that angrily bring Will and Sean to life,' says one reviewer.

'A towering performance by Matt Damon in the lead, and a superlative ensemble led by a terrific Robin Williams, lift Gus Van Sant's emotionally involving psychological drama Good Will Hunting a notch or two above the mainstream therapeutic sensibility of its story,' wrote Emanuel Levy in Variety. 'Centering on a brilliant working-class youngster forced to confront his creative genius and true feelings, this beautifully realised tale is always engaging and often quite touching.' The film has, to date, withstood the test of time: it is now regarded as one of the best of its era, and Damon and

Affleck went on to become megastars.

Williams, for one, was overjoyed. 'A lot of people are coming up to me and thanking me for Good Will Hunting because it meant so much to them,' he said. 'That's just as meaningful to me as someone saying "I laughed my ass off, cuz, y'know, you're one funny bastard."' His performance in the film, people's reaction to it and the Oscar all offered him a sense of validation - that at last he was actually being accepted as a serious actor.

He was, indeed, becoming a more serious character. He was still doing a lot for Christopher Reeve, travelling him to Puerto Rico for an American Paralysis Association benefit and becoming increasingly hesitant to entertain interviewers with his goofy side. 'It's too early,' he grumbled to one, adding, 'I just want to work with characters, with great ensembles of people.' He was, in fact, doing just that, playing Osric in Kenneth Branagh's Hamlet (1996), the tragic story of the Prince of Denmark, and a malevolent bomb-making chemist in The Secret Agent (1996), based on Joseph Conrad's novel. In the midst of a very starry cast, his billing on Hamlet was far lower than usual. Even the minor roles were portrayed by luminaries, including Billy Crystal (another funnyman who wanted to be serious) as First Gravedigger, Judi Dench as Hecuba, Julie Christie as Gertrude, Derek Jacobi as Claudius, Kate Winslet as Ophelia, and Gérard Depardieu as Reynaldo. Marcellus was played by Jack Lemmon. To put it plainly, the cast was diverse.

But Robin was content with a lower billing (albeit being in that audience said a lot) because, to put it frankly, the pressure was off. When your name appears above the credits, your neck is on the line: if the film fails, it will be blamed on you. Williams had a number of flops in his career (one interviewer noted that, while he was willing to confess them, it was clear that he never talked about Popeye anymore), but in circumstances like these, life was a little simpler. He was not required to transport the film.

For he'd realised that huge success comes with enormous pressure; he had his enemies, and there was no shortage of volunteers ready to fling mud if something went wrong. In the 1990s, five of his films - The Birdcage, Jumanji, Mrs. Doubtfire, Aladdin, and Hook - grossed more than $100 million, putting him under additional pressure. He was still showing up unexpectedly at comedy clubs - 'cheaper than therapy' - but he also wanted to be perceived as an homme sérieuse. To emphasise his peculiar position – and add to the strain – he had been dubbed the 'funniest man alive' by both People and Vogue, which obviously led to those claiming they didn't find him that funny.

'They should have just placed a sign on my buttocks that said "Kick me,"' Robin stated. Simply put, he couldn't win.

And, for an homme sérieuse, he did make some questionable cinematic choices. There was Billy Crystal's Father's Day (1997), in which the two actors played men who both believed they were the father of the same boy, with the mother (Nastassja Kinski) lying to both in order to get them to help her find her son.

'For years, Billy and I have been seeking a project to accomplish together. We get along so well on the Comedy Relief specials that it seemed like a natural screen pairing,' added Robin. 'When we're on stage or in front of the camera, it's like two elk showering musk. It's a good rivalry. It keeps our wits about us keen. Every comic is a rival. Denying that is denying the essence of comedy.'

The spirit of comedy, sadly, was not obvious in the film, which sank without trace.

He had a more positive experience in What Dreams May Come (1998), a reference to Hamlet's 'To be or not to be' soliloquy, in which he co-starred with Cuba Gooding Jr. This was an astonishing film, almost metaphysical in its meaning, in which Williams and

Annabella Sciorra played Chris and Annie, a married couple who lose both of their children in a car accident before Chris dies in another. He ascends to Heaven, where he is able to converse with Annie until she commits suicide, overcome by despair. She is therefore doomed to Hell, and despite numerous warnings, Chris descends to rescue her. He initially chooses to stay in Hell with her, but in order to save him, Annie is knocked out of her sorrow, and the two are able to ascend to Heaven once more. They are reunited with their children before being reincarnated and reuniting on Earth.

The video looked fantastic: it proposed the premise that a person's perception of Heaven or Hell is defined by a character's subconscious, and Heaven is spectacular because Annie was an artist who had a great influence on Chris. On the other hand, Hell is so terrifying that some critics felt compelled to forewarn viewers.

That was quite a storyline, and if Robin wanted to be taken seriously, this was the way to go. 'This is a film that, even in its poor state, shows how cinema can conceive the unknown, and can guide our minds into amazing places,' wrote Roger Ebert of the Chicago Sun-Times. 'It also features heartbreakingly effective performances by Robin Williams and Annabella Sciorra,' he added.

But Stephen Holden, writing in The New York Times, was not impressed. 'Not long ago, in Hollywood-speak, love was supposed to imply never having to say you're sorry,' he wrote. 'What Dreams May Come,' one of Hollywood's most intricate metaphysical love stories, introduces a whole new set of obnoxious catchphrases to define the quest for a love that wins over death. These range from the blunt "Never give up," which is repeated like a mantra throughout the film, to foreboding utterances about winning when you lose and losing when you win.' Robin was singled out for special criticism: 'Robin Williams, with his Humpty Dumpty grin and crinkly moist eyes dripping with empathy.'

However, Reelviews' James Berardinelli was favourable. 'Many films have shown paradise and hell, but few have done so with as much passion and creativity as What Dreams May Come,' he remarked. 'The plot, which focuses on the sacrifices one man will make for true love, is neither complicated nor original, yet it becomes a poignant piece of drama because of the director's superb visual sense.'

Meanwhile, Entertainment Weekly's Owen Gleiberman wrote, 'There's a basic contradiction in a fairy tale like this one: the picture may preach to the audience about issues of the spirit, yet its bejewelled special-effects image of the afterlife can't help but come across as aggressively literal-minded.' While reviewers were divided, the public liked it, and the film industry agreed, earning it an Oscar for Best Visual Effects and an Art Directors Guild Award for Excellence in Production Design.

'You feel a lot,' Robin revealed to the Toronto Sun, not just for his part in the film but also for the surrounding interviews. 'There are many feelings, and you wonder, "Do I want to go through this?"" That is the essential question. Finally, I concluded, "Yes!"But dealing with all the loss and pain is difficult." There were just a few days when you could say, "This is a good day." Even while he was in paradise, he struggled with not wanting to let go and trying to connect with her [his wife]. it's difficult to read that and not wonder, "Do I want to go there, to those places?""But what is remarkable is the vision of a highly subjective heaven and hell."

Some of the film was shot in Marin County, near Williams' home, so he could at least return home every night, which kept some of the demons at bay. 'It deals with such emotionally intense issues that I wasn't sure I'd want to do this for four or five months, be near this kind of dark anguish and loss that are at the heart of it,' he told CNN. 'But as we went on, I thought, "Well, it's certainly interesting." And it makes you think about your own life and how you live it - but that's a side consequence of being around such great emotion.'

When he wasn't having to deal with inner anguish, Robin was rather content, not least since he now had an Oscar. 'It's good to have a passport to go anywhere, like Bertolt Brecht stated,' he revealed to CNN. 'It's nice to have that option, to have that kind of opportunity where people say, "You can try this because you've proven you can do a character, a full-on character, a character with this emotional range," because it gives you more opportunities to have comedic roles, which is wonderful, and dramatic roles. It basically provides you with a wider range and a larger playing field.'

However, it had been clear for some time that Williams was as much a serious actor as he was a comedian - 'I go both ways' - and his productivity had remained remarkable. There was a cameo in a somewhat sour Woody Allen film, Deconstructing Harry (1997), a return to clowning in Flubber (1997), in which he played an absent-minded professor, and another serious outing in Jakob the Liar (1999), about Polish Jews during WWII (Robin himself was frequently and incorrectly assumed to be Jewish).

Marsha remained deeply involved in every element of his life, and this is one of the projects on which she worked most closely. Jakob was a former restaurant owner living in a Polish ghetto; his neighbours incorrectly assume he has a radio, and Jakob begins to reassure them by pretending to hear news flashes. The Nazis eventually track out this inmate using a radio and pursue him. The film ended tragically, as was inevitable given the story it depicted. It was originally supposed to be a French movie, but the sensitive subject matter turned off the French producers. It was written and directed by Hungarian filmmaker Peter Kassovitz.

'I then decided to rework the screenplay in English and customise it for Robin Williams,' Kassovitz said in an interview with the Calgary Sun, indicating that the actor was more dependent on Marsha than ever. 'You can't go straight to Robin. You must go through agents and lawyers to reach Marsha, who then chooses whether or not Robin is allowed to receive the content. Marsha has a lot of influence since she has Robin and others want him in their movies, thus Robin relies a lot on her.'

'After reading the script, I met with Peter and we worked on it for nearly a year before I offered it to Robin. 'This is not an unusual circumstance,' Marsha told the Calgary Sun in 1999. 'I spent a year on Mrs. Doubtfire before Robin ever saw the script. I seek for characters that I don't believe he's done before. Much of what producers and writers want Robin to do has already been done. [I treat him] the same as any other actor. I wouldn't consider presenting a screenplay to an actor until it was almost ready for production.'

Robin, for one, was completely content with this arrangement, realising that he could rely on his wife and that, unlike so many of the Hollywood actors he met, she would give him her honest judgement. He described her as "the only person who is brutally honest with me." Most individuals would rather tell me what they believe I want to hear. Marsha, not so much. She won't let me reuse old schtick just because it works. It's critical to have someone who is committed to seeing my development as an actor.'

Given their obvious closeness at the time and how successfully they worked together, the couple's subsequent divorce appears all the more painful. But, despite the fact that Robin was holding it together at the time, staying away from drugs and alcohol and getting into cycling, he was soon to fall dangerously off the rails again.

Patch Adams (1998), on the other hand, was about the last film to help him grow as an actor, and was considered by some to be the bottom of his career. In retrospect, it's easy to see why the project seemed like a good idea at the time: it was based on the true story of Dr Hunter 'Patch' Adams, a doctor with some unusual ideas about how to treat patients. Patch was nearly booted from Virginia Medical School for 'extreme happiness' in the 1990s. Unfortunately, to an objective observer, this discloses the film's flaws at a glance. Patch believes that humour should be utilised to heal patients, but that humour involves dressing up as a clown and setting up a gigantic pair of legs at an obstetrics conference, and while people can be good at either being a doctor or being a clown, few embrace both. Humour can be tasteless and, regrettably, ineffective.

The critics despised it, as did the real Patch Adams, who not only lambasted the picture but also slammed Williams, though he later backtracked on some of his comments. However, star power is star power. Despite receiving multiple Oscar and Golden Globe nominations (none of which were won), the film grossed more than $200 million worldwide. But no one expected the critical reaction, least of all Robin, who gave his regular series of upbeat interviews to promote the film. 'His detractors brand him a modern Don Quixote, but Patch isn't chasing windmills,' he told the Calgary Sun. 'He's committed, dedicated, and clever, and he goes above and beyond to serve his patients.' The doctor entertained cancer patients in one scenario: 'Most of the children in that scene truly are cancer patients,' Robin stated. 'They were cast in the film by the Make-A-Wish Foundation. Their reactions are unplanned. It's not acting.' He also met the genuine Patch, who he describes as "instant friends." He made me laugh so hard that it hurt. He's an outlandish man, a natural clown.' It must have hurt him a lot when his new friend was harshly critical of him after the film came out. But that's show business; those are the breaks.

In another interview, this time with the Toronto Sun, Robin, unknowingly, pinpointed another source of contention in the film. 'We do Patch's medical school time,' he explained. 'It's like the start of this outrageous character. Patch was really upbeat. We make an effort to demonstrate this. But we also show that he can be irritating with his constant urge to disrupt the system.' There is, of course, a risk in portraying someone irritating on screen - it can come off as bothersome.

Williams was now facing another problem: fans, especially those from the early days, were beginning to grumble that they wanted him to be amusing again in the manner he used to be. In reality, he never ceased being amusing - the regular performances in comedy clubs confirmed that, as did his frequent appearances on talk shows, where he seemed to think it was his duty to have people virtually weeping with laughter from the time he got on. But Robin was the clown who wanted to play Hamlet - more than that, he was the clown who could play Hamlet, or Osric, at least. And this was something that he would never totally resolve: comedian or serious actor? And why couldn't people understand he was both?

'People just want to be entertained,' he said to one interviewer. 'They see you do something beautiful and they want you to do it again… and again… and again… until they become weary of it and want somebody else. That's the danger. If you do that again and again and again, they'll finally go, "Harrumph! See that!" But that's what you wanted! "Used to…" And you're dead.' One particular incident with a fan seems to have angered him. 'It's the woman who approached me in the airport and said, "Be zany! Be outrageous!" What? She wants me to be free-spirited. So, like Madonna, you must constantly reinvent yourself. Her Indian year is this year. The Valkyrie year was last year. It was the Edsel-tit year two years ago. What are you going to do? You transform yourself. 'I was released because films like Dead Poets Society, Awakenings, The Fisher King, and Good Will Hunting were successful. It's not only the Academy Award. That perception began some time ago. I changed my career path from comedy to theatre. You're always evolving. So it's just another colour with which to paint.' However, the frustration was evident. Robin could see that he could switch between the two disciplines, so why couldn't anyone else?

Chapter 11.

DECLINE AND FALL

In retrospect, it is evident that 2004 marked the beginning of Williams' long slide. A once-strong marriage was about to crumble, booze and rehab beckoned, and an exceedingly terrible conclusion awaited him. However, there was no indication of this at the time. Looking back, it is also evident that his character looked to splinter. He was dividing his time by then between stand-up and profoundly serious films in which he played not just creeps but even murders. He was no longer making comedy. He was also not his usual animated self when interviewed. If he wasn't putting on the fast-talking crazy act, he was speaking so slowly that he sounded catatonic. Robin the clown still appeared on occasion, but he was accompanied by a more serious persona who could hardly crack a smile, let alone satirise the world's evils. It was a long way from Mork and Mindy.

More bad movies followed, including The Final Cut (2004), a sub-Matrix picture in which he portrayed an 'editor' who edited people's memories. Williams reflected on his dual roles as serious actor and comic. 'It [comedy] gives you a kind of fearlessness because you know that you have to be willing to put your arse on the line to go out and perform it,' he told the Sydney Morning Herald in 2004. 'Directors say they enjoy working with comics because they aren't scared to attempt new things. They must be willing to go to any length to get the laugh. On some level, they are shameless, but also fearless.' But why no more on screen comedies? 'It's difficult to find a script that allows you to kick out that hard, and if you do, people say, "That's not the role, you know."

It couldn't have been easy to gain access to all of this darkness from within. He was also changing physically. Of course, everyone's appearance changes as they age, but Robin appeared to be shrinking. He was approximately half the size he'd been in his twenties when he died a decade later. He was never a snappy dresser, but he began to lose interest in his look, was frequently bearded, and, while not unkempt, appeared to have made little effort to brush up. Although hindsight is a great thing, this is when everything began to alter in his life.

And the cause for this was grief. He had been devastated by his mother's death three years before: 'Marsha and I are both orphans now,' he added. 'I never imagined my parents would pass away. My mother was extremely vibrant. She's a husk the next thing you know. My father, too, nearly died and was brought back to life, and he asked, "Why did you do that?"'"Like many of his generation, he was witnessing his parents survive to extreme old age, with unpleasant consequences. Then he lost them, and his sadness was intense.

And now there was another loss that hit me hard. His close buddy Christopher Reeve was working as a director on an animated feature, Everyone's Hero (2006), when he died suddenly and unexpectedly of heart arrest in October 2004. (Unbelievably, considering their newborn boy, his nonsmoking wife Dana died of lung cancer just two years later.)

Robin was overwhelmed with grief. Any friend's death, at any age, is a difficult cross to bear, but this was a particularly devastating end. Reeve was only fifty-two years old when he died, but his physical deterioration had been heartbreaking to witness. His nine years in a wheelchair had left him a shadow of his former self, virtually unrecognisable from the dazzling Superman. There was no rhyme or reason to any of it: Christopher was a well-liked figure, generous to a fault, and well-regarded. Suffering such a fate felt beyond awful.

'It's difficult for me to realise he's gone because he was such a warrior and such a strong personality and soul to begin with,' Robin told CBS in 2004. 'I recall people coming up to me in New York after the disaster and saying, 'Tell your friend he's fantastic!'Guys on the back of a garbage truck: "Hello, Chris!""There were folks standing outside yesterday while I was coming in for the ceremony. "My thoughts are with you; I'm very sorry for your loss." Just guys, regular individuals giving condolences.

Life continued on, as it always does, but those words couldn't express how much misery he was in. They were more like brothers than pals, as Dana once said. They had started out together when they were young and the world was before them, establishing the relationship that only decades of shared memories can produce. And this is how it was supposed to end. Life was extremely dreary, and no amount of humour, gaming, cycling, or other distractions could drown out the misery that was now engulfing him.

It didn't help that he was making some pretty bad, almost instantly forgettable movies. In The Big White (2005), a travel agent with a Tourette's syndrome wife takes a body and pretends it's his long-lost brother. Not quite Citizen Kane. But, behind the scenes, and despite his apparent anguish, there were acts of pure generosity, not just to the likes of the late Reeve. In 2004, it was reported that he had gone to the bother of calling a dying English Literature instructor named Tim Pechey, whom he had never met but was a huge fan of Robin's work, particularly Dead Poets Society. They first spoke on the phone for thirty minutes before Robin called again and sent him video clips.

This was certainly a habit for Williams. In 2014, shortly after his death, it was revealed that he had recorded a film for a terminally ill twenty-one-year-old girl named Vivian Waller from Auckland, New Zealand, just a few weeks before. 'Hey, girl, what's going on in New Zealand?' said Robin in the video.He even sang a song to her. It was well above what could be expected of anyone, and it occurred just as he was becoming overwhelmed by his own issues.

He also continued his charitable efforts for the armed forces. Robin was back in Afghanistan in December 2004, just two months after Christopher died, as he told the San Francisco Chronicle. 'Some of the Iraqi shows were indoors,' he noted. 'A number of them were outside. It's strange when you're doing the shows, because in Iraq, everyone's in full camo (camouflage) and we're not - so it's kind of like, "Woooow!" It's strange to see all these different camouflages because there's all kinds of camo in the coalition troops, the coalition of the willing." The Australians arrive with desert camo, we have desert camo, and some guys come straight from deployment with full green, which I say, "Doesn't work here." Then there's the Air Force, which has this new blue camouflage. What is this nonsense, unless you're up against the sky? Blue, as in big time. "Like: no," even homosexual folks say. What exactly is a quail egg? It's teal, it's teal and white, it's fantastic!"The shows, we'd perform to 2,000 to 3,000 people in some places... by the end, it got into a good rhythm."

And he was well aware that he was carrying on a tradition begun by Bob Hope during WWII. 'Oh, sure, kind of like a regular Bob Hope performance, except blue,' he explained. 'You know, Bob Hope with a strap-on,' he says. The presentation was launched by the general [Joint Chiefs of Staff Chairman Gen. Richard B. Myers]. He was the hardcore type. He sets the tone simply by saying, "Hey, thank you." Because he gets out and meets everyone, he is very personable. We followed him the first year. We travelled alone the first year. It was just me and the USO shows. We did the shows and stayed in the bases most of the time. We'd stayed, just like in Afghanistan. Bagram, Kandahar, Jacobabad [Pakistan], and finally an Afghan base. You'd go to all of the bases. It's in and out when you go with the general. It was only me the first time. It was nice to work with the general again last year. You travel on his dime and get in and out. There will be no waiting.'

Robin received a Golden Globe Lifetime Achievement Award at the age of fifty-three, probably a little too soon, and voiced Fender in the animated picture Robots (2005). It was a step up, gaining positive reviews and economic success with a cast that included Ewan McGregor, Halle Berry, Greg Kinnear, and Mel Brooks. This was his first animated film since Aladdin, and he enjoyed it. As with the previous film, he improvised, producing almost thirty hours of tape, much of which could not be used due to the material being too blue. 'I believe I have become too adult,' he said. 'I can't help myself. 'I'm inspired, and words just flow off my tongue.'

In the background, however, another major issue was resurfacing: he had gone off the wagon while filming The Big White. He'd been drinking again for a few years, and it was finally taking its toll. 'I was in a small town near the tip of the world, yet you can see it from there, and then I thought: drinking,' he explained to the Guardian. 'I was simply thinking, hey, maybe drinking will help. Because I was lonely and terrified. It was that thing of working so hard and then deciding fuck, maybe that'll help. And it was the most terrible thing in the world.

'You're feeling warm and great. Then, all of a sudden, there's an issue, and you're alone.'

That weakness was showing again: he felt alone and terrified. What had Williams been terrified of? He was still a huge star who could sell out mega-venues and was a strong enough name to get a picture made just on the strength of his involvement. In addition, he had a stable family unit in the backdrop. But the small kid remained, and it appeared that his difficulties were not going away.

In reality, anxieties over his profession were what triggered the initial relapse. He couldn't ignore the reality that his pictures were receiving poor reviews and were performing poorly at the box office. Hollywood might forgive any amount of sentimentality, but it would not accept failure, which was exactly what he was starting to fear. After all, it had happened to many others. Another source of worry for A-listers is the fact that when you reach the top, it's a long way down. There is also no shortage of detractors eager to kick you while you're down.

'The Big White,' Williams said of the movie that got him looting the mini-bars once more. 'It was shot in Skagway, Alaska, a little town. It's not the end of the world, but it's seen from there. The film was intriguing, yet I was concerned. My acting career was not going well. I walked into a store one day and found a small bottle of Jack Daniel's. Then that voice - what I call the "lower power" - says, "Hey. Just a whiff. "Just one." I sipped it, and there was that tiny moment of "Oh, I'm okay!"But it all happened so fast. Within a week, I was going down the street sounding like a wind chime because I was buying so many bottles. I knew it was terrible when they had to take me upstairs on Thanksgiving because I was so inebriated.'

He denied that Christopher Reeve's death exacerbated the situation, but we can't always tell why we act the way we do. 'No,' he told the Guardian, 'it's more selfish than that. It's literally being scared. And you think, hey, this will help with the anxiety. And it doesn't.' What was the source of the dread? 'Everything. It's just an all-around arghhh. It's apprehension and anxiety.'

He realised fairly quickly that this wasn't going to be pretty, yet he persisted for another three years. 'For the first week, you lie to yourself and tell yourself you can stop, but your body kicks back and says no, stop later. It took nearly three years for you to ultimately stop. Most of the time, you simply realise you've started doing embarrassing things.' He recalls drinking at a charity auction given by Sharon Stone in Cannes: 'And I realised I was pretty baked, and I look out and I see all of a sudden a wall of media. "Oh well, I guess it's out now," I say.

At the very least, he avoided the coke. 'I knew that was going to kill me,' he continued. 'No. What wonderful it is to be paranoid and impotent on cocaine! There was no part of me that thought, oh, let's go back to that. Conversations that were pointless till midnight, waking up at daylight feeling like a vampire on a day pass. No.'

But the booze was doing him good. Williams, like many alcoholics, preferred vodka and began having blackouts, unable to recall what he had said or done the previous day.

By 2006, his life was in disarray, and his marriage was in serious jeopardy. 'You know, I was shameful, and you do stuff that makes people disgusted, and it's difficult to recover from,' he said later. 'You can say "I forgive you" and all that, but it isn't the same as healing from it. Under family pressure, he entered into rehab, specifically Oregon's Hazelden Springbrook treatment centre, where he stayed for two months, drying out. He was also concerned about what had happened to Mel Gibson, another actor who had spent decades battling alcoholism and had recently been arrested for driving under the influence - he was naturally anxious that something similar could happen to him. Locals who saw him throughout his visit described him as quiet and dishevelled. He was obviously in a foul mood.

In truth, he was far sicker than he had realised. 'Williams began a 30-day treatment program,' a source told the Sun. 'However, after the initial 30 days, he realised he needed another 30 days of inpatient therapy to get his life under control. He spent the last 30 days at a residence near the rehab centre that was specifically designed for after-care patients. He was still compelled to attend daily AA meetings and consultations with his therapists.' After he departed, he did not return to the family home, instead renting an apartment in Los Angeles. 'Instead of returning to his wife and two teenage children in Napa Valley, he's relocated to Los Angeles, where he's renting an apartment and living with a "sober companion," according to the source. 'Williams hired the buddy to keep an eye on him 24 hours a day and make sure he doesn't go off the wagon.' He was still expecting to save his relationship with Marsha at the time, but it was not to be.

In 2006, he told Good Morning America, "It waits." 'It waits for the moment when you think, "It's fine now, I'm OK," and then, all of a sudden, it's not OK. "Where am I?" you wonder. I didn't realise I was in Cleveland."' The treatment stint was enough to get him sober again (albeit not for two decades - there would be a lapse), but the damage had already been done, and his marriage was beyond repair. Finally, the personal and professional partnership that had worked so well was coming to an end.

Williams managed to keep working in the midst of it all. He was still concerned about his career, and he was no longer being offered the kind of jobs he'd had in the past, but his output remained consistent. House of D (2004), directed by David Duchovny (and starring his daughter Zelda), came next. It portrayed the story of Tommy, a thirteen-year-old boy, and his friend Pappass (Williams), a middle-aged guy with the same mental age as Tommy. The attempt to stop playing damaged children trapped in an older man's body was not working well. The picture, ominously described as a "coming-of-age comedy drama," was, however, another flop. He could have used an even break at this point in the game.

Nonetheless, like a consummate professional, Williams did interviews to publicise the project. In 2005, he told Cinema Confidential, "I just did the research about a high-functioning mentally handicapped." 'Socially adept, but intellectually and emotionally not that adept in certain situations, intellectually about a ten- or eleven-year-old, and physically capable of doing manual labour and stuff... People who know, who say, "I know what that is," and others who look around and say, "Oh, that's different." He's very verbal, but he's slow with other things. He can understand and pick up on what's going on emotionally, but it's a halted development at a certain time, maybe around ten or eleven.' And, as he didn't mention, 'again'.

But it was great joy working with Zelda, who played Melissa, Tommy's love interest. Her father was very pleased. 'She was so good in House of D,' he exclaimed happily. 'She was very intuitive. I was playing a psychologically impaired character. I'm kind of sitting there watching her and thinking to myself, "She's good." She possesses the same level of cerebral agility, but she is extremely sensitive. The best compliment of all was that she was not just a good actor, but also a nice person. She was kind to all the other youngsters. She ate lunch with everyone else. She didn't have an attitude with them and was pleasant to everyone on the staff. People stated, "Your daughter is good, but she is also nice."

Then there was 2006's The Night Listener. It's based on the original book by Armistead Maupin (of Tales of the City fame) and tells the story of a DJ who meets a young child over the phone but begins to doubt his existence. It was again another mixed bag. Listening to interviews from the time, Williams sounds much more sombre, even when he can't stop himself and starts putting on goofy voices again. But he was now hinting at much bigger issues as well. 'Do I sometimes perform in a frenzied manner? Yes,' he said to Terry Goss on the radio. 'Am I constantly manic? No. Do I ever cry? Oh, yes. Does it have a strong impact on me? Oh, no, no serious depression. No. I get down, as I believe many of us do at times. You look around and exclaim, "Whoa!"At times, you look around and think, 'Oh, things are OK.'''

His parents' deaths, the death of his buddy Christopher Reeve, drinking, rehab, and now a failing marriage... He was now stuck in a vortex that seemed to be spinning out of control at moments. Then there was the inescapable fact that his career had not been what it should have been: he had made some fairly bad movies, and no one seemed to want to forget it. 'Why?'The Guardian inquired. Why had he made this decision?

Williams made a brief comeback. 'Well, I've had a number of people tell me they enjoyed seeing Old Dogs with their kids,' he said. 'No, it covered the bills. To make money, you sometimes have to make a movie. You completely understand what you're getting yourself into. You know they're going to screw it up. And that's all right.' But was it truly OK? He was, after all, a Juilliard-trained actor who took his art seriously. And quite a few people in the audience thought it was completely unacceptable. When you've had your fill of grandeur, it's difficult to accept second best.

Unfortunately, more trash followed - Man of the Year with Christopher Walken (2006), RV (also 2006), which only lasted a couple of months in theatres before moving straight to DVD - all of the pain of previous years may have influenced his judgement in that he participated in so much that was so terrible. Perhaps it was because another pricey divorce was on the horizon, but in 2004 and 2005, he appeared in three films each, while in 2006, he appeared in an astounding six pictures. That's a lot of labour, and either he needed the money or he was using the work to distract himself from what else was wrong in his life. Something was going on, in any case, yet among all the forgettable flicks, certain gems showed hints of standing the test of time. Though not his own vehicles, they benefited greatly from his input.

The first of these was Night At The Museum (2006), which was a Ben Stiller vehicle (if Williams hated playing second fiddle to a younger comic actor who was playing a character that he himself might have been given a few years earlier, he had the good judgement not to say it). Larry Daley, a security guard at the American Museum of Natural History, discovers that the displays come to life at night, played by Stiller. Theodore Roosevelt (Robin) explains why this is happening, and Larry gradually learns how to regulate the chaos. The film garnered mixed reviews, but it was a big commercial success, and it was credited with increasing visitors to the genuine American Museum of Natural History. Robin was not a fan of sequels, but he was set to act in two more for this picture, one of which has yet to be produced.

Happy Feet (2006), the second project, also produced a sequel. Robin voiced Ramón and Lovelace in this animated film about penguins. It was ostensibly a romp, but with a strong environmental message: 'You can't make a narrative about Antarctica and the penguins without bringing that dimension,' director George Miller said. Not only did the film receive positive reviews, but it also dethroned Casino Royale, featuring Daniel Craig as the current incarnation of James Bond, at the box office. It also received numerous honours, including an Academy Award for Best Animated Film.

Robin reprised his role in the sequel (unimaginatively titled Happy Feet Two, 2011), and, whether he likes sequels or not, this series prompted a serious discussion about the environment, which continues to this day. It's strange that a man so often accused of overt sentimentality ended up in a picture that appeared to be a children's entertainment but was actually a much more serious discourse.

More films followed, not always noteworthy, but he couldn't avoid the inevitable any longer, regardless of his workload. The three-year drinking spree had taken its toll, and Marsha's estrangement was complete. Robin, the dependent youngster who couldn't stand being alone, was on his way to his second divorce.

Chapter 12.

A FRESH START?

Williams may have hoped to repair his marriage, but there was too much stress to deal with, and Marsha filed for divorce in March 2008, citing irreconcilable differences. He was to end up with a £20 million bill - no joke, even for someone who was extremely wealthy. 'I get along great with my ex-partners, even if we're no longer together. And they always appreciated my body hair, which was obviously a bonus,' he told the Daily Telegraph, clearly trying to make light of the situation.

In actuality, there was much more going on. Robin equated marrying a comic to owning a cobra. 'Basically, there's some novelty, and the fun is showing the cobra to your pals - but cartoons can be unpleasant,' he said. 'In addition to our acute insecurity, we are occasionally equipped to be nasty.'

But, all jokes aside, this was no laughing matter. Marsha had been a great source of stability for Robin: four years after they met, he told the New York Times in 2008, 'I don't need to go out to a club today and receive a little bit of closeness from 100 or 200 people. 'I can get that chatting to pals around the table now.' She had done so. His ex-wife had also aided in the development of his career, and while it hadn't fared well in recent years, she had been extensively involved in projects such as Mrs. Doubtfire and Robin Williams Live On Broadway. They had worked together on the Windfall Foundation, organised countless fundraisers, and supported each other in their respective charity endeavours, Marsha's specific causes being Doctors Without Borders and Seacology. She was also the mother of two of his children and had previously assisted him when he was in a difficult situation.

Robin was being married for the third time, and it would be incorrect to suggest that Susan Schneider, his third wife, mattered less to him than Marsha. But his divorce from Marsha was a watershed moment in his life. They had shared not just his reign at the top of the Hollywood A-list, but also the sorrow of his first divorce and the joys of family life. Marsha had been the centre of Robin's existence for two decades, and their divorce was a devastating blow. At the heart of it, he was deeply unhappy and insecure, and it occurred at a time when his career was stagnant. This was not an ideal situation.

Despite the fact that neither had said anything publicly, there had been hints for some time that all was not well. Marsha was not there when Williams received the Peter J. Owens Award from the San Francisco International Film Festival in 2007. She made a very kind speech following Robin's death, but there was definitely a lot of hurt on both sides. He was now in his mid-fifties and had to deal with the issue of ageing (which was not easy for anyone). 'I don't really think about old age,' he insisted, according to Philippine News Online. I recognize that at a certain age, there are things that you suddenly realise you didn't hear. Or you have a senior moment and ask yourself, "What is my name?" Robin, Robin, Robin. Yeah, exactly.' Life was proving to be extraordinarily difficult.

To make matters worse, Robin's older half-brother, Robert Todd Williams - 'Toad' - died in 2007 as a result of complications from heart surgery (which he would subsequently endure). There was yet another reason for Robin's distress: while the three half-brothers had not been close as children, they had grown so as adults, and Robin was devastated. Toad ran Toad Hollow, a famous winery, named one of his saloons Risky Liver Inn (in private, at least!), and, as Robin said of him, 'Toad left a big footprint with a cork, or as a friend said, he left a great trail.' A larger-than-life bon viveur, he would be greatly missed.

By this time, Christopher Reeve's widow Dana had also died, another tragedy that left Williams speechless, not least since she had left behind a small kid. So he did what he always did when life looked to be getting the best of him: he went back to stand-up comedy. In 2008, he launched a twenty-six-city stand-up tour titled Weapons Of Self Destruction, a clear reference to his recent troubles. Many additional dates were added, and the tour extended to the United Kingdom and Australia. There was some speculation that he was doing it for the money, but whatever the truth was, certain factors stood out. The first was that stand-up had always provided some form of shelter in difficult circumstances, and those were really difficult times.

Billy Crystal, an old friend of his, agreed. 'Over the last few years and the trauma that he's been through, his brain has been the one thing that's kept him buoyant,' he told The Guardian in 2009. 'I think he needs the stand-up in a different manner than he did before. It's still a secure place for him to be, but now he can talk about things and make himself feel better rather than just everyone else.'

The second was that, despite his difficulties in his film career, his stand-up act was as popular as it had ever been. The tour sold out almost immediately - not bad for a man in his late fifties. Williams the film actor was in trouble, but Williams the stand-up comic remained as popular as ever. This was always the case: popular admiration for Robin was unwavering till the end of his life.

It was something he noticed when he was out on the road. 'I just strolled around, and most people said, "Oh, hello, how are you?""I told the Robin Williams Fansite,' he said. 'Ninety-nine percent of the folks are really nice.

'The only people I encounter who cross that line are drunks. And, having been one myself, I understand, but I don't have to endure it. I was strolling... he wasn't even intoxicated. There was a guy who suddenly started grabbing me to take a picture with his cell phone, and I yelled, "Let go." He kept squeezing me, and I said, "No, no, I know your English isn't great, but don't grab me." Treat me like a person, not a prop. And the majority of people do it.'

It was an indication of his inability to remain nameless, which he had lived with for years. But it also meant that when he had problems, he had to make them very public.

The tour began in September 2008, with Robin openly admitting that he was doing it for money because he did not like the film parts he was being offered. Among the typical targets, he publicly discussed his recent travels ('Poor me, poor me... bring me a glass!') but even this was not as simple as it seems. 'I've always felt that Robin's lightning speed and flash of wit was an effort at concealing, rather than disclosing,' observed comic Eric Idle, who had known him for a long time. 'He'd be talking about something intimate or sexual, but it was always in broad strokes, not about him.'

He had certainly lost none of his infamous hostility to George W. Bush - 'The Bush library will be interactive - which is code for, Not So Many Books' - and was happy to talk about the new President as well: 'Obama is an amazing combination of Martin Luther King and Spock.' And he was just as funny as ever; he still had the ability to bring audiences to tears of laughter. He didn't have to cope with actual life on stage, as he frequently commented.

But, if he was doing this tour to distract himself from his current problems, life was about to throw another one at him. As the tour progressed, he began to endure moments of breathlessness, which is not surprising for an act as fast-paced as his. Offstage, he was quieter, but on stage, he was still the firebrand he had always been, and by February and March of the following year, he had developed a cough as well. He went to see his doctor as it became clear that something was wrong. He appeared to have a respiratory problem at first, but it soon became evident that the issue was with his heart. An angiography revealed that he needed a cardiac bypass, so he went in for surgery at the Cleveland Clinic in Ohio in March 2009, after postponing some tour dates, before returning home for a few weeks to recover. He had one of his aortas replaced with a cow's valve, which became the basis for many more jokes.

'I'd end gigs and then realise, "Wow, I'm really kind of rundown," he told the New Zealand Herald. 'It wasn't like I was weary but feeling terrific,' she says. So I was in Miami, set to do some shows, when I got the call, "No, no, you have to get this checked out." You have two weeks to determine where you want the surgery to take place." That was like saying, "Beep! Put on the brakes and do the valve grind," which seems like a terrific sexual dance to me. "You've got to do something about this, pal," the tour basically said.

Joking was second nature to Robin. In truth, it only served to heighten his sense of melancholy. He had 'a little of worry' that the surgery might kill him, he told The New York Times in 2009, adding, 'I suppose, literally, because you have shattered the chest, you are vulnerable, entirely, for the first time since birth. It's like, oh, don't cry now. My little ones! 'My children.'

In the end, the procedure was a complete success, but it could not have happened at a worse time. He'd already been having a rough time, which he was dealing with by being on stage, and having to sit at home with only his thoughts for company wasn't going to make him happy. He wanted to work and he needed to be out there, so it was a huge relief when he was allowed to travel again.

Williams, on the other hand, was eager to demonstrate that he was back on track. Eight weeks after the operation, he posted a photo of himself with his T-shirt pulled up, revealing a massive scar that spanned the entire length of his chest. He subsequently appeared on David Letterman's show to explain what had occurred to him, interspersed with a few riffs. 'I realise now that shortness of breath is kind of code for cardiac trouble, just like weariness is code for alcoholism,' he said. Yes, I'm visiting Betty Ford because I'm tired. I'm going to take a nap!

'I have an ethanol problem. I'd walk up a flight of steps and suddenly realise, "I'm old." But something was wrong, so I went in, where they performed a stress test and I walked on the treadmill. I have one new valve and one that has been repaired. I have a cow valve, and the grazing has been enjoyable. I also provide a wonderful quarter cream. It comes from a cow's heart. They give you the option of having a pig valve and then finding truffles, or a cow valve and then finding truffles. Mechanical valves are substantially more durable. It's fantastic, but if someone uses a remote control, you fart.' Oh, and, 'It really helps you appreciate the little things, like breathing.' That was Robin, and he was back on the road.

'I took three months off and after that I was like, "I think I can do this,"' he told Star Adviser. 'One night, perhaps a month or two into the rehabilitation period, I walked on stage and I was out of breath and I said, "Not ready, not ready." After three months, I said, "No, I can do it." I'm slightly slower than I was before, but not by much. Only a few people will notice, but you are going a little slower.'

He'd spend a lot of time touring, with the act inevitably ending up as an HBO special, and despite his complaints about the quality of the job being provided, the films kept coming. And it's not accurate to say they were all bad. 'I've been doing tiny films,' he explained to the New Zealand Herald. 'Small films are fun to make, but they don't pay the bills. Literally. You do things, and they're fantastic, and I'm extremely proud of you, but they don't pay the bills. Even the director of the last film I worked on, Bobcat Goldthwait, is a comic. He has to go out to clubs. I'm performing in auditoriums. We're both making money the traditional way.'

And what about the duds, he was asked? 'You don't lament them. There are some that you think to yourself, "Maybe you shouldn't have made that," but you did. There are some that are fantastic, some that aren't so great, and some that make you exclaim "Woah!"And usually, the ones that didn't work were the ones where someone said, 'This is going to be a smash.' That is the most terrifying one - when you went in with the wrong motivation - to make shitloads of money.'

There it was again, that connection to money. Despite the early conjecture following Williams' death, it does not appear that he was in financial difficulty, expensive as his divorces had been, not least because he still had a few films to release. What is more plausible is that he was growing preoccupied with the idea of running out of money, which is why he talked about it so much. However, once you enter a period of darkness, everything appears bleak, even if he wasn't quite there yet.

That project he mentioned working on with Goldthwait was, in reality, a huge return to form. The two of them collaborated on World's Greatest Dad, which was on par with some of his previous works and received some of his greatest reviews in years. It only had a limited theatrical distribution as a small, art-house film, but it showed him at his sharpest, a world away from his more romantic fare. It was a comedy, but it was a very dark comedy. Robin portrayed Lance, an English literature teacher who was the polar opposite of his character in Dead Poets Society since he taught a poetry class that everyone despised. He was a single dad to his unpleasant kid Kyle (Daryl Sabara) and engaged in a desultory romance with a colleague teacher, who was simultaneously dating a significantly more successful teacher at the school.

Lance gets home one night to find Kyle had accidently murdered himself through auto-erotic asphyxiation, and in order to save his son's disgrace, he pretends to have hung himself the traditional way, as well as creating a suicide note. This note, as well as Kyle's notebook, which Lance has forged, become cult items at the school.

Lance himself has a significant transformation: his students begin to admire him, and he appears on television as the media becomes increasingly interested in the narrative. The only person who suspects Kyle is his friend Andrew (Evan Martin), who believes the moving note and journal are out of character for his pal. When the principal reveals that the school library will be renamed after Kyle, Lance can't stand it any longer and admits his crime. He is free while being despised by everyone.

Patch Adams it was not, but it was a significant return to form. If Williams had stuck to pictures like this, he would have faced far less criticism than some of his other selections - even if, as he conceded, the film was never going to be a large money maker - since people enjoyed it. The film World's Greatest Dad premiered at the Sundance Film Festival in Utah. The judgement was 'lusciously wicked and refreshingly creative comedy that tackles love, loss, and our odd search for fame,' with Robin receiving plaudits for his superb performance. The critics praised it as "brilliant," "genius," and "one of the best films of the year."

'A stunningly good dark comedy about the power of favourable posthumous publicity. 'One of the year's must-see films,' wrote Catherine Bray. 'Goldthwait's rhythm is unsteady, and his humour is frequently "off," but the sense of dangerous provocation is gripping,' The Independent's Anthony Quinn wrote. And the message was clear: Williams was still capable. If only he would pick his other endeavours more carefully. However, and there was a significant but, the picture was not a huge hit, very definitely due to the subject matter.

Goldthwait approached Robin as a friend, not as a potential lead, to see if he might assist him in getting the project into production. 'I read it to say, "Look, let me see if I can help you get this made for you." Because when he did "Shakes the Clown", I played Jerry the Mime as a favour, and it was like, let me see what I can play... and then I thought, "No, this is really good."

He was conscious, however, that they were dealing with a sensitive subject. 'I can't imagine dealing with the loss of a child... so that's impossible to imagine. But the script was gutsy, so we had to go with it. You can't be dismissive. You can't say, "Hey, my kid was a jerk." He's no longer alive. What is the point?" You can't go that way." Then there came the cleaning scene... "Yeah, and clean up after his kid." And even the thought of zipping up his fly and throwing away every scrap of evidence makes me think, "Okay, how are we going to deal with this, coach?"''

Things appeared to be improving. Robin had recently married Susan Schneider, whom he met in an Apple Store. 'I was wearing camouflage pants at the time, and she asked, "How's that camouflage working?""I answered, "Pretty good, since you noticed." I got this funny sensation, so I added, "I know this sounds like a terrible pickup line, but I feel like I know you." She said, "Yeah, me too." And then we found we had a common theme in sobriety,' he told People Magazine. They'd met in 2009, just before Robin learned he'd require surgery, and Susan, a San Francisco-based graphic designer, had shown to be a keeper, caring for him as he recovered. She was a painter, fifteen years his junior and five inches taller, and she brought some much-needed enjoyment back into his life.

They married in 2011 at the Meadowood Resort in St Helena, California, after a brief courtship, then honeymooned in Paris. Williams was a man in need of female companionship: he'd never had any trouble attracting women, but he needed something more stable than a few meaningless flings.

'No way, Apple. 'A-p-p-l-e store; we were both hunting for bizarre technology and our eyes met, and we just got married last month, which, given my track record, is a bit like bringing a burns sufferer to a fireworks exhibition,' he told the Daily Telegraph on another occasion. 'I've done the ranch thing, now I'm doing the water thing where I go kayaking and paddleboarding and take to the woods for hours on my bike,' Robin said. It's my time, and it's quite soothing. Because I am confident in my sexuality, I also have a gay rescue pug named Leonard, whom I take for walks. He has a boyfriend, and the two of them are preparing to adopt a Siamese kitten. We're quite modern.'

It was a new family, and you didn't have to be a psychologist to figure out that Robin was probably trying to replace the one he had lost.

However, he continued to be concerned about money. 'I've never been approached to appear on I'm a Celebrity... Get Me Out of Here!' she says.'So I assume I mustn't be on the professional skids just yet,' he pondered, according to the Daily Telegraph. Besides, I'd never appear on it. Never. I'm not good with snakes and I can't dance. In fact, I am such a lousy dancer that I could only ever appear on a telethon to raise money for injured people: "The phone lines are open. Pledge us money and we'll make him stop."' He appeared to have confused I'm a Celebrity... with Strictly Come Dancing, but the worry was evident.

The increased stability in his personal life, along with the fact that he was making some decent pictures, seemed to have opened the door for Williams to take a chance. Years had passed since his underwhelming performance in Waiting For Godot at the Lincoln Center, but in 2011, he made his Broadway debut in Rajiv Joseph's Bengal Tiger at the Baghdad Zoo at the Richard Rodgers Theatre. His manager's wife, David Steinberg, had introduced him to the play. Robin played the tiger, a beast kept by two American soldiers in the early days of the Iraq war. He was heavily bearded (a look he wore a lot back then). The tiger addresses the audience and continues to do so even after a soldier shoots and kills it. Bengal Tiger was a brave play, and the actor who played it was also brave. Again, he received rave reviews.

'But Mr Williams, the hyperactive comic with a marshmallowy streak in films, never indulges the audience's appetite for exhibitions of funny ingenuity or pinpricks of poignancy,' said Charles Isherwood in The New York Times. 'He gives a performance of focused intelligence and integrity, embodying the animal who becomes the play's questioning conscience with a savage bite that never loosens its grip.' This was, in fact, significantly better than his Godot days: he was finally receiving the professional acclaim he craved.

'It just hit me hard,' Robin told The New York Times. 'I read it and thought, "I'm in." I can come in and build it from the ground up." I'm also hairy enough to be a tiger, so that's a plus. To put it bluntly, most of the characters are ghosts. I mean, I don't want to give anything away - 'This is what it's about' - but right off the bat, you're in Iraq, and there are all these ghosts strolling around, conversing and becoming more cognizant as the play progresses.'

Of course, he had gone to Iraq before, entertaining US troops. 'The last time I was [in Iraq], I slept in [Saddam Hussein's son] Uday's hunting lodge, even though all he hunted was Russian whores,' he told TIME Magazine in 2011. 'It was as tacky as if Hitler had built Graceland. Even Colombian drug barons are thinking, "This is some tacky stuff." But my views about the battle are about ghosts. I was just there a few weeks ago, and [everything] is "winding down." What do you leave behind when it all ends? "The Americans think when something dies, that's it, it's over." But when you go to the Middle East, you discover there's a real sense that things stay around.

It was, in fact, a triumph, and he garnered widespread praise. He was proving time and again that he still had it in whatever profession he touched. But Robin's financial instability persisted, and he decided to sell his lovely Marin County ranch in order to earn a steady income.

Chapter 13.

SHADOWS FALL

Williams kept adjusting to his new existence. His children had grown up and left home, though their base had always been with Marsha in the aftermath of the divorce, so it was just Robin, Susan, and the dogs. He used to like the chaos of the family, but even if he and Marsha hadn't divorced, life was changing. He was getting older, and life was moving at a different speed for him.

In 2011, he told MSN Today, "It's quiet." 'I just saw Zelda, my daughter, the other night. My oldest son is married, and my youngest son has recently graduated from college. They appear to have deviated from Earth's gravity, and I am observing them. "There he goes!"' I'm really proud of myself. I don't have a college degree, and neither does my father, so when my son, Zachary, graduated from college, I exclaimed, "My boy's got learnin'!"

Of course, the incredibly learned Robin had a lot of knowledge.

He was also proud of his children. 'I have to thank my ex, Marsha,' he told Parade. 'She was responsible for most of the work on that level. She tries hard to ground and protect them, but not too hard. I was fairly out for three years when I started drinking. Now it's up to me to be there for them. The most important thing to say is, "If you need me, I'm here." Zelda's acting and writing are both excellent. Cody is a music producer. Zachary is married and employed. It was one of the most touching days of my life when he graduated from NYU. I was really pleased with him. Because I lack a college diploma.'

It seemed strange that Robin was obsessed with this now: perhaps he had reached a point in his life where he was pondering over what might have been.

Meanwhile, the films kept coming in. In Happy Feet Two (2011), he resumed his dual role: 'Well, you have to do it better than the first time to make it worthwhile, not simply for the sake of the franchise,' he told MSN Today. '[Director] George [Miller] gave it his all. I asked him what he thought after he saw it, and he said, "Well, I don't know, but I think it's better." I responded, "I think so, too." He used the technology, performances, and everything to take it to a new level.'

'There was one moment as Lovelace when I started speaking in tongues,' he remarked. I went completely insane and almost passed out. "That's fantastic," George said. Continue your efforts!" I told him that if I kept going, I'd collapse. I've only recently begun this Baptist hymnal thing. "Hmmmm Hmmmm Hmmmm." I believe that's what inspired the gospel music in the film.'

Then there was The Angriest Man in Brooklyn (2014), which was not one of his finger picks. The plot revolves around an annoying man who is involved in a vehicle accident and is so disrespectful to the doctor at the hospital where he is sent that she tells him he has just ninety minutes to live. Queue the patient rushing around the place, attempting to right the wrongs he has committed in record time, while the doctor, fearful of being struck off, charges around, attempting to locate him.

The reviews were harsh. Variety described the film as "a schmaltz opera that indulges Robin Williams' most melancholy tics and themes." In New York Magazine/Vulture, Bilge Ebiri wrote, "The film never quite manages to figure out what it's actually about." 'The film is obviously emotional at its core, but it's also meant to be funny, thanks in part to Mr Williams's energetic but ultimately futile attempt to portray a jerk,' wrote Nicolas Rapold in The New York Times. 'Every moment between two people comes across as drunkenly shot video of a play rehearsal gone catastrophically wrong,' Robert Abele wrote in The Los Angeles Times.

'Robin Williams once again proves he can insufferably turn the energy to 11 without blinking,' remarked Drew Hunt of Slant Magazine. 'As outlandish as Williams becomes in these sequences, it's not entirely his fault. 'He's acting out a screenplay by Daniel Taplitz that's filled with terrible writerly flourishes,' said AV Club's Jesse Hassenger.

Ouch! This was not a pleasant read for a rather sensitive man.

Along with the brickbats, there were plenty of bouquets thrown at Williams. He was invited to an event honouring him at The Paley Center for Media, which was sponsored by TV Guide.

'I never think of myself as a legend,' Robin remarked, puzzled. 'It's a strange label, like "mythological," with little people behind you shouting, "We worship you." When I first started in television, there were just three networks; now there are hundreds. And, despite the fact that this is my first visit to The Paley Center, I know you can come here and see wonderful television from the past.'

Bobcat Goldthwait, the director, delivered a speech. 'I referred to Robin's new wife as a MILF during my toast at his wedding,' he claimed. 'And I threw him a bachelor party, when a wonderful performer dubbed Lady Monster walked up and set fire to various areas of her body. It was the least I could do for Robin, who has always offered me a shoulder to cry on when things became tough. We've had a good run as best friends.'

More small-scale films followed, such as The Face of Love (2013), in which a lady, Nikki (Annette Bening), falls in love with someone who looks eerily similar to her late husband (Ed Harris). Robin portrayed Roger, a good friend who aspired to be more.

The filmmakers were overjoyed to have Williams on board: 'He's certainly one of my favourite individuals I've ever worked with,' producer Bonnie Curtis remarked. 'I met Robin when I was about twenty-three or twenty-four. We worked together on the film Hook [1991], which had a three-year filming schedule, so we all got to know one other very well. I called Robin because I assumed he'd just hire this man for this part.'

She handed him the script, and he called me and said, "Well, now Ed has the really good part," to which I agreed, "Yes, he does." Robin then continued, "But I get this guy." I have Roger, and I know I can do it. "At the very least, I'd like to try." And that was the end of it. He was just adorable. He told me that he based it on an actual incident that happened to his mother, seeing a man who looked precisely like his father and how that affected her, and that he'd developed it from that, which is quite lovely. The tone is extremely pleasant. There is immense depth and melancholy at the same time. This is a highly intense and palpable thing.'

There was nothing wrong with creating this type of film - it was art-house territory, with a fascinating plot, and was well worth making - but it wasn't the mega-bucks blockbuster of yesteryear, and Williams had worked himself up into a frenzy over money. Life was also pretty sad in other ways. Williams offered a kind tribute to his buddy, comedian and actor Jonathan Winters, in the way that so many of his contemporaries would soon do for him as well.

'My mentor was Jonathan Winters. When I told him that, he said, "Please." "I prefer 'Idol.'" But I knew it had to be real. I recognized him the instant Jack Paar handed him a stick on The Tonight Show. What happened next was the work of a genius. John and his stick changed into a dozen distinct personalities, each with their own sound effects - a fly-fisherman, a matador, Bing Crosby playing golf... he was a comedy at the speed of thought, and I was fascinated.

'Twenty years later, I was cast as Jonathan's father on Mork & Mindy. On our show, his riffs were like gigantic mini-movies. I would occasionally join in, and jamming with Jonathan was like dancing with Fred Astaire. He always brought out the best in you.

'The beauty of Jonathan was that he was a huge, intelligent kid who never grew up and saw the world as his playground. Johnny switched off the lights in April, but he sure burned bright while he was here. Big dude, thanks for the spark.'

But that wasn't the only piece of bad news. Robin was still an avid cyclist, but his longtime friend Lance Armstrong had become embroiled in a drugs scandal after it was discovered that he had been using illegal performance-enhancing chemicals.

'I got into cycling because I couldn't run anymore,' Robin explained to Parade in 2013. 'I liked jogging, but everything hurt so badly all of a sudden. I began cycling after Zelda was born. I was already a cycling aficionado before I met Lance. I followed his team on five Tours de France. That's why it was so upsetting when [the doping scandal] broke.'

Do you think he felt betrayed? 'It wasn't just Lance, either. The majority of the team was doping. I haven't seen him since one of the most recent Livestrong benefits, which I believe was immediately before the Oprah interview. This general impression that the dream was gone was truly like a wake for someone who was still alive.'

The television industry was in a frenzy. Picket Fences, Chicago Hope, The Practice, Ally McBeal, and Boston Legal creator David E. Kelley was launching a new series, The Crazy Ones, about a man named Simon Roberts who works in advertising with his daughter Sydney at a Chicago agency called Lewis, Roberts + Roberts. There was a lot of anticipation because the man who would play Simon would be none other than Robin Williams. The portion was written specifically for him. It was his first appearance in a television series since Mork & Mindy thirty-one years before.

Sarah Michelle Gellar, who plays his daughter Sydney, clearly thought it was a huge thing. She called a friend of hers, Sarah de Sa Rego, who happens to be married to Bobcat Goldthwait, as soon as she heard Williams would be starring in a new series to say she wanted to play Sydney. Gellar claims she's talked to' Robin: 'I even contacted his best friend and I was like, "I have to be on this show." Please notify Robin!" I truly did!'She explained. Her request was granted. 'He is legendary! Consider this: the greatest stand-up comic of all time, an Academy Award winner, and the nicest man on the planet,' Gellar remarked.

'It's as if Gandhi performed stand-up!' Robin replied.

He had utilised television, like so many others before him, to establish a cinematic career: did this feel like a step back? There was no reason for it to feel that way. It was becoming more normal for prominent movie actors to appear on television; Alec Baldwin, for example, had been a revelation in NBC's 30 Rock. And David E. Kelley was a household name in television. There was no reason to be concerned.

'We needed an actor who could communicate genius, craziness, and comedy while keeping humanity in mind,' Kelley told Parade magazine. 'Robin was my first and only option.'

Robin was clearly having a good time. He sounded really thrilled about his temporary relocation to Los Angeles with Susan. 'It's a lot of fun,' he told Parade. 'I'm having a great time doing it with Sarah. She's a lovely lady. And I've done some research on the father-daughter bond because I have a daughter. You know, pride and trying to help her along while not assisting so much that she doesn't learn.'

But there was something else he liked about it as well. 'Having a solid job is tempting,' Robin admitted bluntly in 2013. 'I have two [alternative] options: go on the road performing stand-up, or do little, indie films nearly on the cheap [minimum union salary]. The films are excellent, yet they frequently lack distribution. Bills must be paid. In a nice way, my life has shrunk. I'm selling the Napa ranch. I simply cannot afford it any longer.'

The ranch didn't sell, and it stayed unsold after his death, but there was a truly unpleasant note running through all of this, and, while Williams had long fought with melancholy, it came out as manic humour, not feeling wretched. 'If you think you're hot, you're not,' he explained. People fling themselves at you when you're hot. A cop once stopped me and said, "Hi, Mr. Williams. I'm not going to issue you a ticket, but I have a film idea."' And what about when you're not so hot? 'People go away from you,' he said, sounding gloomy.

Regardless, he was ready to give it his best. Simon, his persona, was described as "a guy who can sell anything." He could sell Starbucks frappuccinos. He could sell God clouds. Simon is a complex character. He's been living hard and on the edge for a long time. Multiple marriages, rehabilitation, and even rehabilitation in wine country. Trust me, I did the research myself.' The concept was that Simon had been married and divorced several times, neglecting Sydney as a child, and was now determined to make amends as an adult - though she would have to prove herself to him before he would take her on. Simon was the crazed one, while Sydney was his rock.

More regular personalities appeared, not least to offer Sydney a love interest and to foster a competitive spirit. Pam Dawber, nicknamed Mindy, appeared as a guest star near the end of the season, marking the first time she and Robin had appeared together since the old days. So, how did the new series fare? No, despite the fact that all of the ingredients were present.

Everyone involved admitted to being nervous. Zap2it inquired about

Robin and Sarah's relationship. 'Very beautifully,' he commented. 'I believe we were really honest on the first day. I leaned over and said, "I'm a little afraid," and she answered, "Me, too." Knowing there was no audience relieved the strain, and we began doing it.'

What about James Wolk, who portrayed womanising copywriter Zach Cropper? 'He's quite good,' Robin responded. 'It's good for him to let loose and be as outrageous and humorous as he can while playing this studly persona. "Did you have sex with her?"" "Not yet." "OK, nice." They can also pitch with me, throw ideas around, and send him in as the designated schtick man, which is sort of fantastic.'

Were the younger actors put off by his improvisation? 'Oh, no, they keep up, and they're faster than me,' Robin claimed. 'They're just as fast, if not faster. For me, at 62, I need to establish my rhythms and get back up to speed. "OK, oh, it's over," I thought at the end of the pilot. Now I have to get back into shape, rediscover the character, and rediscover the moments. How daring can you go?"'

However, that was not the entire story; read on for more.

To put it mildly, the evaluations were mixed. 'Williams can't help but revert to his old tricks on occasion - cartoon voices, gurning, rambling wordplay - but there's a decent amount of pathos to his performance as part-buffoon, part-genius Simon Roberts as well, and the comedy veteran shares a warm, genuine chemistry with his onscreen offspring Gellar,' said Morgan Jeffery of Digital Spy.

Meanwhile, the Pittsburgh Post-Gazette Rob Owen was keeping an open mind: 'Whether The Crazy Ones can come together as a series over time is an unanswered question, but the pilot offers enough charm and wit to deserve future consideration.'

'I don't know how it does it, but The Crazy Ones continues to be one of the most boring comedies with one of the most fantastic casts on television today,' said Ross Bonaime of Paste. The entire program is basically "meh." It also feels like this show operates in a vacuum, with nothing in any previous episode having any effect on anything that comes after it. There are no ongoing plot arcs, nor are there any actual characters with whom to connect.'

'The Crazy Ones, created and executive produced by David E. Kelley, stars Williams as advertising genius Simon Roberts, while Gellar plays his daughter Sydney, who also happens to be his business partner,' writes Kelly West for Cinemablend.com. 'Roberts is lively and outlandish in just the way you'd expect from Williams' regularly riffing funny man, while Sydney is a touch more reserved, not always keen to go along with her father's lightning-fast line of thinking and ridiculous behaviour.'

The Boston Herald undoubtedly got it right when it said, 'Williams looked weary.'

He could have been fatigued, given that the never-ending stream of flicks had not stopped. Even his superhuman vitality had to have limits now that he was in his sixties. But there was also the impression that he was giving up. He'd had a terrible few years, and the sadness that was never far away had enslaved him once more.

Worse, he was drinking again, according to some others. One scene was taken at Wolfgang Puck, a well-known watering hangout in Beverly Hills, the birthplace of the power lunch. 'Robin insisted on a proper drink,' a person stated. 'No one had ever seen him drink before. One drink led to another, but it seemed to settle him down.' If this was true, it was bad news: not only was he drinking again, but he wasn't even trying to hide it. When he went off the wagon in 2003, he tried to hide his activities by telling bartenders he was ordering drinks for someone else. He didn't seem to care who knew 10 years later.

There were also other issues. Williams was selected because he was zany and spontaneous, but when he began doing the same on set, it was rumoured that the rest of the actors couldn't handle it. Sarah Michelle Gellar, in particular, was claimed to have found it extremely difficult to work in this manner, however it should be noted that she has never spoken publicly about this and was deeply saddened to learn of his death. And it was nothing like Mork and Mindy. Robin had been a highly ambitious and charming twenty-something keen to make his mark at the time. He was now in his sixties, and what you can get away with in your twenties doesn't often work several decades later. He was moaning about the lack of chemistry in the cast, and his feelings were shared. Cast members muttered about his neediness and his attempts to be the centre of attention. It had worked with Mork before, but not with Simon.

He also caused controversy by bringing his rescue pug, Leonard, to the scene. 'He brought it everywhere with him,' said the insider. 'When he wasn't filming a scene, he was holding, petting, and gushing over the dog,' some said.

Overall, the event was becoming a very miserable experience, which was reflected in the viewership figures. It began with 15.52 million viewers, the highest-rated premiere that autumn, but dropped to 5.23 million by the series finale. Williams was nominated for several accolades for his performance but did not win any. Sarah Michelle Gellar, on the other hand, won the People's Choice Award for Favourite Actress in a New TV Series, which may have been rather disappointing.

The cancellation of the show was announced in May 2014. So that was his return on television. Not exactly the triumphant return that everyone had hoped for. And it was a heartbreaking blow for a man who was already struggling to cope.

He was back in recovery in July of that year. 'After working back-to-back projects, Robin is just taking the opportunity to fine-tune and focus on his continuous dedication, of which he remains quite proud,' said a statement. But everyone around him could see that something was extremely wrong. He had been worried about his film career for years, his television comeback had failed, and he was struggling to keep on track, according to some.

He'd spent his entire life fighting them off, and suddenly he was swamped by them. When people reach that point, they lose sight of the fact that they have the support of a family behind them. Robin simply didn't realise how much he was loved, as his daughter would later observe.

Chapter 14.

EPILOGUE: A COMEDIC GENIUS

Nobody knows what finally drives someone over the brink. Robin Williams had fallen into a horrible melancholy, but while job setbacks probably played a role, he had been dealing with depression his entire life. Health and financial issues didn't help, but what happened to him was the culmination of a prolonged fight, not a series of failures that left him depressed. And, as his daughter Zelda stated after his death, he had no idea how deeply he was loved. Even those who had claimed to loathe him in his prime were moved to tears when they learnt of his demise. However, Williams transformed the face of light entertainment. He may have made some shaky films, but he also made several outstanding ones that have become part of our popular culture. Even Mork & Mindy, a lighthearted television sitcom, is remembered fondly by a generation. And he was the greatest stand-up comedian of his generation, an artist no one could compete with and someone who could send entire theatre audiences to helpless, weeping laughter. But having the energy to do so always indicates a darker side. In some ways, his attempt to tame his wilder side could be perceived as having a negative impact on himself.

'It's been a series,' he told Rolling Stone in 1991. People commented on Good Morning, Vietnam, "Ah, at last he's found a way to be funny while remaining a little restrained." They said to themselves, "Oh, this is interesting - he's even more restrained." And when it comes to Awakenings, it'll be "Look! He's been medicated! He's even gone beyond. What will he do next? He's pretending to be a door." And then what? 'It's a black hole.'

Without becoming an amateur psychologist, he eventually slipped into that black hole, as did a lot of other excellent comedians who were eventually flattened by a world with which they could not cope. Robin was sometimes accused of being overly sentimental: this may be true, but being overly sensitive is more likely. 'Williams seemed to have an extraordinary aptitude and susceptibility to take on so many personas,' says the author. According to Dwight DeWerth-Pallmeyer, associate professor of communication studies at Widener University in Chester, Pennsylvania. 'Williams was able to cognitively delve inside characters in a subtle way that showed both the complexity of the characters he played and his own intelligence,' says the critic. But doing so made him even more vulnerable: if he was playing a damaged character, he had to feel that damage himself. And he was severely harmed. He never stopped portraying the man-child because he was the man-child. Even his clearly mature activities, such as narcotics and the occasional bout of promiscuity, stemmed from an inner neediness. He had some debauched times in his life, to be sure, but he was not a debauched man himself. 'There was also a depth of humanity in his work, an understanding of what it means to be different, and how everyone has a creative and generous side - he thoroughly understood and explored the impulse to connect with others at a very basic level, something that the best entertainers know how to tap into in order to speak about larger truths,' said one reviewer. Derek A. Burrill, associate professor of Media and Cultural Studies at UC Riverside in California, told the Christian Science Monitor that Williams has 'that particular something' like Tom Hanks, Bill Cosby, Peter Sellers, and Richard Pryor.

Williams also revolutionised the face of stand-up comedy, becoming a highly influential character in San Francisco's burgeoning comedy scene and launching a new free-flying improvised style. He impacted an entire generation of aspiring comedians, including Jim Carrey, who used to make Mork impressions. And when it came to humour, few could compete with his level of energy and sense of anarchy. His legacy will undoubtedly live on.

And all of his agonising over his career was unnecessary; he was one of the most successful actors of his generation. According to Box Office Mojo, his films have grossed a total of $3.2 billion in the United States and $5.2 billion globally. He's appeared in thirteen films that have grossed more than $100 million in the United States, which is impressive by any standard. And he would have gotten even more money from DVD sales and rentals. The main plum roles may have dried up, but he stayed at the top for thirty years, significantly longer than all but a handful of actors. Many younger comedians who were the hottest thing in town for a few years have now been mostly forgotten, but Robin Williams hasn't, as evidenced by the outpouring of grief after he died.

Williams' continued standing as a powerful Hollywood figure was underlined by the fact that, at the time of his death on August 11, 2014, he had three films scheduled for release. A Merry Friggin' Christmas, about an estranged father and son on a road trip together; Night At The Museum: Secret Of The Tomb, in which he reprised his role as Theodore Roosevelt in the popular franchise's second sequel; and Absolutely Anything, a sci-fi tale starring Simon Pegg and Kate Beckinsale in which he voices an animated dog named Dennis. Boulevard is another art-house film that has yet to be released as of this writing. The never-ending talks regarding a Mrs. Doubtfire sequel have also resumed, albeit in the aftermath of his death, it seemed unlikely to happen. After Robin's death, director Chris Columbus told Variety, "His performances were unlike anything any of us had ever seen; they came from some spiritual and otherworldly place." He was definitely one of the few people who deserved to be called a "genius,'" he remarked. Given that lineup, it appears that his financial issues were all in his head. Perhaps it was his age that did him in. He was in his sixties - no age these days - but Hollywood is constantly looking for the new and Robin couldn't be considered that. But he was a true original, a hugely brilliant man who could switch from stand-up to serious, as well as a kind-hearted and giving person. Although the famous Robin Williams is no longer with us, his light will continue to shine for many years to come.

Printed in Great Britain
by Amazon

59863398R00090